Smoke on the Mountain

An Interpretation of the Ten Commandments

JOY DAVIDMAN

Foreword by
C. S. LEWIS

THE WESTMINSTER PRESS
PHILADELPHIA

Copyright © 1953, 1954, by Joy Davidman

C. S. Lewis's foreword reproduced by permission of
Curtis Brown Ltd, London, on behalf of C. S. Lewis Pte
Ltd.

Published by The Westminster Press®
Philadelphia, Pennsylvania

PRINTED IN THE UNITED STATES OF AMERICA
9   8   7

Library of Congress Cataloging in Publication Data

Davidman, Joy.
  Smoke on the mountain.

  1. Ten commandments. I. Title.
BV4655.D32 1985   241.5′2   85-7622
ISBN 0-664-24680-X (pbk.)

To
C. S. Lewis

CONTENTS

FOREWORD

Joy Davidman, who began her career, appropriately enough, as nursery governess to a lion-cub, first came before the public as the poetess of *Letter to a Comrade*, which won the Yale Series of Younger Poets award for 1938. The volume showed, side by side with a delicate precision of imagery (one remembers the crabs "jointed, Japanese, and frail") an occasional orotundity, a deep bell-like note, not very typical of its period; in "The Empress Changes Lovers" and "Absolution" it successfully answered the question we must put to all young poets: "Can you go beyond the pageant of your bleeding heart and the general state of the world, and present a *situation*?" They all date from her Communist period.

How she got into the Party and how she got out again she has described in a beautifully balanced little essay, "The Longest Way Round," contributed to Dr. Soper's *These Found the Way* (1951). The adult convert to Christianity is of course a characteristic figure of our age. Joy Davidman is one who comes to us from the second generation of unbelief; her parents, Jewish in blood, "rationalists" by conviction. This makes her approach extremely interesting to the reclaimed apostates of my own generation; the daring paradoxes of our youth were the stale platitudes of hers. "Life is only an electrochemical reaction. Love, art, and altruism are only sex. The universe is only matter. Matter is only energy. I forget what I said energy is only"; thus she describes the philosophy with which she started life. How, from the very first, it failed to accommodate her actual experience, how, as a result of this discrepancy, she was for some years almost "two people," how Communism, too, broke up under the impact of realities more formidable even than itself, must be read in her own words. Re-reading the poems in the light of the essay one is struck by a recurring image; that of the brain within the skull as within a fortress which may, or may not, be held against "the universe." The essay describes exactly how "the universe"—indeed, something much more important than it—broke in. For of course every story of conversion is the story of a blessed defeat.

Another point of interest in Joy Davidman's work comes from her race. In a sense the converted Jew is the only normal human being in the world. To him, in the first instance, the promises were made, and he has availed himself of them. He calls Abraham his father by hereditary right as well as by divine courtesy.

He has taken the whole syllabus in order, as it was set; eaten the dinner according to the menu. Everyone else is, from one point of view, a special case, dealt with under emergency regulations. To us Christians the unconverted Jew (I mean no offence) must appear as a Christian *manqué*; someone very carefully prepared for a certain destiny and then missing it. And we ourselves, we christened gentiles, are after all the graft, the wild vine, possessing "joys not promised to our birth"; though perhaps we do not think of this so often as we might. And when the Jew does come in, he brings with him into the fold dispositions different from, and complementary of, ours; as St. Paul envisages in Ephesians ii. 14-19.

Before she became a Christian, even before she had (temporarily) considered the possibility of Judaism as a religion, Joy Davidman was keenly aware of this difference in the blood. In one poem, there is a suggestion that the whole "Aryan" *ethos* could be regarded as a "clinging fog." I suppose when Elijah on Carmel cried out "How long halt ye between two opinions?" he was dissipating a fog. I suppose we Northerners, pagan, romantic and polytheistic in grain, are a kind of people of the mist when seen from the dreadfully unambiguous standpoint of Israel. If "fog" is too severe a word, at least it is no severer than what she says of her own people; "My root Who evolve viciously in the east." Not perhaps viciously, but without doubt fiercely—I cannot help here remembering the lion's governess. The finer spirit of that fierceness, if one must describe it in an abstract noun, is presumably what our fathers called *zeal* (a word disquietingly absent from the Christian vocabulary these last hundred years or so). But it is best grasped not in an abstraction but in an image, in that glorious, sustained image from the XIXth Psalm where the Sun and the Law became fused in the poet's mind, both rejoicing, both like a giant, like a bridegroom, both "undefiled," "clean," "right," and "there is nothing hid from the heat thereof." One sees the whole desert landscape—no rock nor hillock large enough to throw a shadow in which one could hide from that tyrannous, disinfectant blaze.

Something of that old Hebraic quality has gone into the book to which I am writing this preface. First there is the style. I do not of course mean that Joy Davidman's style is derived from her blood. It comes, like all good writing, from an individual talent, from reading, and from discipline. But how well it fits the theme!

Many writers on "religion" (how odious a word, by the way, how seldom used in Scripture, how hard to imagine on the lips of Our Lord!) have a positive love for the smudgy and the polysyllabic. They write as though they believed (in the words of the late George Gordon) "that thought should be clothed in pure wool." There is no wool here. The author, to be sure, is an American and uses her own language, not always lexically or idiomatically the same as ours; but it is none the worse for that. A test comes in chapter nine where she quotes a great rocky piece of sheer sense from Johnson which would have instantly shown up any vagueness or fustian in its neighbourhood if such had existed, and comes off unscathed. She even dares to lay a stone on top of that grim cairn and it is worthy of its place. ("The pay is bigger nowadays—but then, so are the lies.") For the Jewish fierceness, being here also modern and feminine, can be very quiet; the paw looked as if it were velveted, till we felt the scratch. At the opening of chapter nine, where we English may perhaps feel that some withers are more wrung than our own, the apparent innocence which puts us off with Titus Oates is an example. So, in another passage, is that much needed coinage "others-denial."

Secondly, there is the very theme of the book. What should a Jewish Christian write on if not the Law? But notice that the choice of subject means no relapse into mere Judaism, nothing that need alarm the most Pauline of us. The author knows quite as well as any of us that Mr. Legality will never bring us to the Celestial City and has got over the fallacies of Moralism fairly early in life. She had good opportunities for studying it at close quarters. She knows that only love can fulfil the Law. That, I think, is the answer to a criticism which someone is sure to make of this book; that in most of its chapters we have much more about diagnosis than about cure. In reality, of course, a "cure" in the sense of some recipe added at the end of each chapter— some "law to be a fence about the Law" and inevitably breeding more Law—is not really being offered at all. The author is not a quack with a nostrum. She can only point, as in her concluding chapter she does point, to the true Cure; a Person, not a set of instructions. Pending that, she is no more inhibited than her ancestors about diagnosis; one might frankly say, about denunciation. A Jeremiad? But should we never read Jeremiads? If it comes to that, should we never read Jeremiah himself? The Canon judges otherwise.

The sins of the Americans (for whom, in the first instance, the book was written) are doubtless not exactly the same as our own. Many of their sins, indeed, we are now hardly in a position to commit. Hence, inevitably, there are passages in this book which English readers may make a bad use of, reading them with complacent self-congratulation. But in the main it is a true bill against all Western civilization. The flaw in us which Joy Davidman seems to me to expose with most certainty will be to some perhaps an unexpected one: the sin of fear, not in Donne's sense but, quite simply, cowardice. Hence she can speak of one minority as being "protected by a fortunate illiteracy from the bombardment of fear propaganda." I am doubtful whether many readers, after reflection, will be prepared to give her the lie. It may be true that great nations have never before faced a greater danger; but have great nations ever met danger with such an appearance of poltroonery? Perhaps it is only appearance. Perhaps, if the moment comes, our bite will prove better than our howls. If not, we shall have to confess that two millennia of Christianity have not yet brought us up to the level of the Stoics and Vikings. For the worst (according to the flesh) that a Christian need face is to die in Christ and rise in Christ; some were content to die, and not to rise, with Father Odin.

I have ventured to use the word "denunciations." This must not be taken to mean anything wild or indiscriminate. On the contrary the quality in this book which, I anticipate, will stand out more clearly the better it is known, is precisely the union of passionate heat with an intelligence which, in that passion, still modifies and distinguishes and tempers. Notice (what I especially value, because it supplies a corrective which I especially needed) how after exposing what is banal, meretricious, and greedy in the popular idea of "Progress," our author unexpectedly, and truly, points out what pure and noble elements originally contributed to that idea. Notice, again, how while admitting the sins worse than murder she shows how disastrously the concept "worse than murder" can be used to confuse and etiolate the reality of murder itself.

I do not of course agree with Miss Davidman at every point. In such a book every reader will have his own crow to pluck with the author. For my own part, what I would most gladly see altered are certain passages where she quotes myself for thoughts which she needed no sense save her own to reach and no pen save her own to express. But every old tutor (and I was not even that to Miss Davidman) knows that those pupils who needed our assistance least are generally also those who acknowledge it most largely.

C. S. LEWIS

INTRODUCTION

THE SIN OF FEAR

And all the people saw the thunderings, and the lightnings, and the noise of the trumpet, and the mountain smoking: and when the people saw it, they removed, and stood afar off. . . . And Moses said unto the people, Fear not: for God is come to prove you, and that his fear may be before your faces, that ye sin not. And the people stood afar off, and Moses drew near unto the thick darkness where God was.

—Ex. 20:18, 20, 21.

THERE IS a tale told of a missionary in a dark corner of Africa where the men had a habit of filing their teeth to sharp points. He was hard at work trying to convert a native chief. Now the chief was very old, and the missionary was very Old Testament — his version of Christianity leaned heavily on thou-shalt-not's. The savage listened patiently.

"I do not understand," he said at last. "You tell me that I must not take my neighbor's wife."

"That's right," said the missionary.

"Or his ivory, or his oxen."

"Quite right."

"And I must not dance the war dance and then ambush him on the trail and kill him."

"Absolutely right!"

"But I cannot do any of these things!" said the savage regretfully. "I am too old. To be old and to be Christian, they are the same thing!"

Not a very funny story, perhaps; there is too bitter a point in the laugh. For, if all the truth were told, how many of us, in our hearts, share the cannibal's confusion?

13

How many thousands, in this America, picture Christianity as something old, sapless, joyless, mumbling in the chimney corner and casting sour looks at the young people's fun? How many think of religion as the enemy of life and the flesh and the pleasures of the flesh; a foe to all love and all delight? How many unconsciously conceive of God as rather like the famous lady who said, "Find out what the baby's doing and make him stop"?

That is, how many of us both inside the Church and out have reduced the good news out of Nazareth to a list of thou-shalt-not's?

Quite a few, doubtless, or we should not always be worrying and teasing at the Decalogue and making reinterpretations like this one. Nor should we have so many materialist writers who talk sneeringly of "religionists" and their outdated superstitions which interfere so unscientifically with man's fine, free gratification of his natural instincts (a term which in this context usually means only *one* instinct). True enough, we are having a religious revival at the moment. We are crying out to be rescued from the deadly terrors of the world we have made. Peace of mind, peace of soul, peace of heart — our spiritual leaders promise them all, and we, for whom there is no peace, snatch at them in our bewilderment and despair. God, for many of us, is a life preserver flung to a drowning man.

And so he is, if you happen to be drowning. But you can't drown all the time. Sooner or later you have to start merely living again; you reach shore, splutter the water out of your lungs — and then what? Throw away the life preserver? If your interest in God is based upon fear rather than love, very likely. In such a case, you will be willing to pay very high for that life preserver as you go down for the third time; you will offer for it all your worldly treasures, your lusts and greeds and vanities and hates. But once safely on shore, you may be minded to throw it away and snatch your treasures back.

We are in danger of forgetting that God is not only a comfort but a joy. He is the source of all pleasures; he is fun and light and laughter, and we are meant to enjoy him. Otherwise our Christianity is no better than the cannibal's. We shall try to be negatively good, and make a virtue of misery; plume ourselves on the rejection of delights for which we are too weak, measure our piety by the number of pleasures we prohibit. And others will react against us by rejecting religion altogether, probably announcing with pride that they are choosing "life" instead. Saint Augustine phrased the Christian law as: "Have charity and do what you like." The modern materialist often makes it simply: "Do what you like," and then rushes off to ask his psychoanalyst why he no longer seems to like anything. Whereas the Pharisee, alas, tends to invert Augustine into: "Neither do what you like *nor* have charity."

Either way, this is not the good news but a counsel of despair and defeat, at best of escape. This is not the law of Moses but a meaningless law of fear. "Thou shalt not enjoy life" was never Christ's teaching; it is we who have brought our terror and impotence into religion, and then accused religion of bringing it to us. For we live in an age of fear, and we have infected our very faith with our paralysis, as certain previous ages infected it with their cruelty. No wonder the Decalogue makes us uncomfortable. We have turned it from a thrilling affirmation into a dull denial.

Yet there was the sound of trumpets in it once.

When Sinai flamed and thundered, the Children of Israel were indeed briefly afraid. Apparently nothing short of a volcano, however, could intimidate them long enough to make them re-examine the code by which they lived. They were lusty and lustful men; they heartily enjoyed their hewings and smitings and woman-stealings; and if they got killed on their forays — well, if you sat in the tent and worried about *that* you were as good as dead already. A safe life was unthinkable to them — nobody had ever told them that they were entitled to social security. Even the love of God which was entering their hearts was no gentle thing, but the fierce love of a strong man for a stronger master.

The discovery that he was a God of justice must have given

them a profound spiritual shock; it seemed, then, that there were things a man *shouldn't* enjoy!

Shock; and also exultation, for the Decalogue raised them above the trivial level of enjoyment, gave life a shape, a purpose, a plan. Though previous Eastern cultures had struggled upward temporarily to some knowledge that justice pleased the gods, it is on the thunderstone of the Tablets that Western civilization has built its house. If the house is tottering today, we can scarcely steady it by pulling the foundation out from under.

When civilization caught up with the fierce Israelites, it happened that they got the worst of it; for their settled life, crushed between greater nations, was less fortunate than their savage life had been. A conquering and rejoicing people declined into a conquered and wailing one. The sins of the animal — blind enjoyment of the present moment — were replaced by the sins of the devil: bitterness and pride, with a rejection of the present and a desperate attempt to play God by getting control of the future; in short, the sin of fear.

All this while the scribes and Pharisees were busy multiplying interpretations of the law. To keep the Sabbath holy, ultimately, meant obeying 1,521 different blue laws — for example, you had to remove your false teeth. To keep the name of God holy, you had to give up using it altogether; eventually its very syllables were forgotten. The frightened men of Christ's day, groaning under the intolerable social security of the Roman peace, turned to their law and found only a tangle of gobbledygook. Like us, they could obey it blindly or reject it blindly; but they could not possibly make sense of it. Something new had to be added for that. And, again like us, they did not want negative commandments at all. They wanted a positive law, to put some heart back into them. They could not get it from the scribes and Pharisees; nor, for that matter, from their neighbors the skeptical Greek philosophers and scientists; nor from the Roman theorists of law and government. Nor can we.

Negative, feeble, old — according to our critics, our Western culture is all this and worse. And indeed in a materialist society people are *born* old. Flesh-and-blood grandfathers and grandmothers are not our problem. True, we have more of them than we used to, so many that they are becoming a special medical study and a new political power. Yet, if all were well, that should be our gain. In a healthy nation Grandmother's smiling wisdom ought to balance Granddaughter's reckless and restless energy; Grandfather's serene detachment should offset the youthful passion of Grandson. But what if there is no deep youthful passion? What if Grandson, in the Army at twenty, complains over the loss of Mom's cooking and the tame desk job? What if Granddaughter, married a year or so, finds beating up cake batter too great a task for her slack muscles and fretful mind? What if the highest ambition of youth is to be *safe?*

Ecclesiastes has summed it up for us:

". . . The years draw nigh, when thou shalt say, I have no pleasure in them; . . . also when they shall be afraid of that which is high, and fears shall be in the way, and the grasshopper shall be a burden, and desire shall fail: because man goeth to his long home, and the mourners go about the streets."

Fears shall be in the way, and desire shall fail. To the spiritually old, however young and strong their bodies, death seems lurking around every corner, and fear sits by their bedside and grins at them. Any minute now, the atom bomb will drop or the bacterial warfare begin, and we shall go to our long home; and since most of us are at least half materialists, we suspect that it will be a very long and dark home indeed. The frightened man cannot use his strength or his youth; he is in the position of the old African chief. What's the good of saying to *him*, " Thou shalt not "? He can't, anyway. What's the good of warning *him* against excessive enjoyment of this world? He would give everything he possesses for the power to enjoy this world genuinely, lightheartedly, fearlessly, for five minutes. And he can't.

Fear is so much our disease that we have forgotten it is a disease; we take it for granted as the normal basis of all human actions. Our UN delegate, with no sense of anything shameful in the confession, declares that fear is the root of Western foreign policy. Our Army assumes that vast numbers of its casualties will be fear cases; there will be too many atheists in foxholes. Our advertising men base half their art of money-making upon fear. Our psychiatrists found an entire theory of our misbehavior on it, telling us that the holdup killer shoots, not out of a desire for money, but out of fear of the slum; that the wayward girl picks up men, not out of sexual desire, but because she's afraid of her father; that the spoiled child throws tantrums, not because he can't have the toy he wants, but because he's terrified that Mother doesn't love him. Whether or not such interpretations are true, they reveal the mental state of the age that accepts them — an age when, for many, fears are in the way and desire has failed.

Not the whole picture, of course! Perhaps the great majority of men go on as they always have — stumbling, cursing, but on the whole enjoying themselves. There are still *healthy* sinners among us, people who get so much out of this life that they are in danger of forgetting the next. There are still lovers who enjoy sexuality, soldiers who enjoy the adventure of fighting, and even, perhaps, rich men who enjoy money. Many are still protected by a fortunate illiteracy from the bombardment of fear propaganda which our books and magazines and newspapers are hurling at us. And there are always the saints, the men and women so close to God that no temporal disaster can shake their eternal joy.

But the articulate, the leaders of opinion, the policy makers, all those who set the tone of our society, seem for the most part to be frightened men. And how do frightened men deal with life?

They don't; they run away from it. The simplest among us flee openly, rushing from woman to woman, from drink to drink, from one empty amusement to another, wondering why they get so little contentment out of the eighty-miles-an-hour joy ride from unloved Here to unrewarding There. Some of us are prouder; we conceal our fear under hate, and bully

Negroes or persecute political heretics or nag our children. Some of us are subtler — we deny fear altogether, pretend that terror is an illusion and that safety through "science" is just around the corner. This last escape is often the way of the intellectuals, the world thinkers, the worriers among us. Often the worrier tries to persuade himself that his own death won't matter, as long as the nation or Western civilization or the human race survives — only to become, mysteriously, ten times as worried as before; with each new headline he dies a thousand deaths.

The real trouble with the Ten Commandments today seems to be that we frequently manage to obey most of them without much difficulty, not from virtue but from lack of the animal energy to break them. To the African who was too old, to the American who is too worried, the Ten Commandments seem at first glance irrelevant. We clamor like Christ's contemporaries for a new, a modern restatement, a positive interpretation in the terms of our own time; and we fail to see that we already have it. We have had it for two thousand years. The positive form of the Decalogue is in the Sermon on the Mount. And at the very core of it are the words: "Take therefore no thought for the morrow." That is, better translated: "Don't worry about the future."

The words of Jesus are timeless. What worked for other frightened men will work for us. But our society refuses to listen; this injunction about tomorrow is precisely the one thing we will not accept. Our whole economic system, our civilization, our American way, is built on worrying about the future! Our life is based on fear; if we should ever grow brave, what on earth would become of us?

Even in church, we worry about world problems we cannot understand or master, and we waste our time and substance on committees whose announced purpose is to save the world and whose real purpose turns out to be getting some politician elected. Even in church, we are so shaky in our faith in the next world that we often talk as if the teachings and promises of our Lord were a mere convenience for putting *this* world to rights. And some of our preachers, with the best intentions, keep announcing plans for "bringing Jesus up to date."

Well, but mustn't the churches adapt Christianity to suit the ideas of our time? No, they must not. Our ideas are killing us spiritually. When your child swallows poison, you don't sit around thinking of ways to adapt his constitution to a poisonous diet. You give him an emetic.

Therefore the answer is still the old answer: "Perfect love casteth out fear." We do not need a world in which there is nothing to be afraid of — in which obeying the law would be easy. Nor can we have such a world, for all our strivings; no matter how pleasant and safe we make the journey, the end of it is death. What we *do* need is to remember that we have been redeemed from death and the fear of death, and at rather a high price too. Our generation has never seen a man crucified except in sugary religious art; but it was not a sweet sight, and few of us would dare to have a real picture of a crucifixion on our bedroom walls. A crucified slave beside the Roman road screamed until his voice died and then hung, a filthy, festering clot of flies, sometimes for days — a living man whose hands and feet were swollen masses of gangrenous meat. That is what our Lord took upon himself, "that through death he might destroy him that had the power of death, that is, the devil; and deliver them, who through fear of death were all their lifetime subject to bondage."

"Thou shalt not" is the beginning of wisdom. But the end of wisdom, the new law, is "Thou shalt." To be Christian is to be old? Not a bit of it. To be Christian is to be reborn, and free, and unafraid, and immortally young.

I

GOD COMES FIRST

I am the Lord thy God. . . . Thou shalt have no other gods before me.

— Ex. 20:2, 3.

"Hear, O Israel; The Lord our God is one Lord!"

What a surprise! What an incredible thing to say!

Everyone knew that the universe was a wild and chaotic thing, a jungle of warring powers: wind against water, sun against moon, male against female, life against death. There was a god of the spring planting and another god of the harvest, a spirit who put fish into fishermen's nets and a being who specialized in the care of women in childbirth; and at best there was an uneasy truce among all these, at worst a battle. Now along comes a fool, from an insignificant tribe of desert wanderers, and shouts that all these processes are one process from a single source, that the obvious many are the unthinkable One!

Whoever he was, he shouted it so loud that it has echoed down all time. From the minarets where the muezzin cries that God is God; from the synagogues where the cantor calls in sonorous and unchanged Hebrew; from the churches of Christendom, the voice is the same, and the word the same. The universe is one process, created by one Maker.

It was the greatest discovery ever made.

Scholars are not sure who first phrased it; perhaps the tribal hero Moses, perhaps the idealist Pharaoh Akhnaton, more likely a host of nameless God-haunted men slowly working it out over the centuries. However it came, it is the fundamental assumption of modern science as well as that of timeless religion. And however it came, the belief in one God slew a

21

host of horrors: malign storm demons, evil jinn of sickness, blighters of the harvest, unholy tyrants over life and death; belief in God destroyed the fetishes, the totems, the beast-headed bullies of old time. It laid the ax to sacred trees watered by the blood of virgins, it smashed the child-eating furnaces of Moloch, and toppled the gem-encrusted statues of the peevish divinities halfheartedly served by Greece and Rome.

The old gods fought among themselves, loved and hated without reason, demanded unspeakable bribes and meaningless flatteries. While they were worshiped, a moral law was impossible, for what pleased one deity would offend another. If your wife ran away from you, it was not because you beat her, but because you'd forgotten the monthly sacrifice to Ishtar; just offer a double sacrifice, and you'd get two new wives prettier than the old.

Then came the knowledge of God. An almost unimaginable person — a single being, creator of heaven and earth, not to be bribed with golden images or children burned alive; loving only righteousness. A Being who demanded your whole heart.

In the scalding bitterness of the Babylonian Exile, Jehovah's prophets saw, not a victory for the enemy's gods, but the justice of their own. Nebuchadnezzar was merely the scourge with which God punished his people for their sins. With that concept a God-ordered universe was envisioned, and men set about accepting the moral law of the Decalogue — a shining rainbow bridge stretching between earth and heaven.

Yesterday's thrilling discovery, however, may be today's tame commonplace, and when men have heard a statement too often, they grow incapable of hearing it at all. So with the idea of one God. Why shout it in our ears again? we ask fretfully, turning in our sleep. Have we not accepted it since childhood? Except in that dark underworld of the mind where dwell astrologers and numerologists and cash-on-the-barrelhead psychics, nobody really believes in many-god notions any more. Why tell us what we know?

Perhaps because we know it only with our lips, not with

our hearts. With some of us, the question is not One against many, but One against none. The old pagans had to choose between a brilliant, jangling, irresponsible, chaotic universe, alive with lawless powers, and the serene and ordered universe of God and law. We modern pagans have to choose between that divine order, and the gray, dead, irresponsible, chaotic universe of atheism. And the tragedy is that we may make that choice without knowing it — not by clear conviction but by vague drifting, not by denying God, but by losing interest in him.

A nominal deist will say: "Yes, of course there must be some sort of Force that created the galaxy. But it's childish to imagine that It has any personal relation to me!" In that belief atheism exists as an undiagnosed disease. The man who says, "One God," and does not *care,* is an atheist in his heart. The man who speaks of God and will not recognize the presence of God burning in his mind as Moses recognized him in the burning bush — that man is an atheist, though he speak with the tongues of men and of angels, and appear in his pew every Sunday, and make large contributions to the church.

We live in an age of lost faith and lost hope and empty hearts. Today the Commandment, "Thou shalt have no other gods before me," must include, "Thou shalt have me."

For the beast gods have come creeping back. If we will not have the One, we must in the end accept the many after all. A man with nothing to worship is a man in a vacuum, and the false gods will rush in. They are not idols nowadays — not Dagon of the Philistines or "the brutish gods of Nile." They are worse things. The ancient image worshipers were, at least, worshiping something not themselves, a Power greater than themselves; they were trying in their limited way to make an image of God, and when the image proved faulty they could break it and make a better one, until the day came when they needed no image at all. But the false gods of today are things of the spirit, and as hard to pluck forth as it is hard for a man to pluck out his right eye. The beast in the heart is always the self.

In the last analysis there are only two things to worship —

the true power and the false power; God or devil; God or self. The primitive mumbo-jumbo worshiper was often serving God in intention. The modern monotheist is frequently adoring his own image in the mirror.

It is true that few of us can worship the self naked and unashamed for very long. For one thing, it simply doesn't work. Living for his own pleasure is the least pleasurable thing a man can do; if his neighbors don't kill him in disgust, he will die slowly of boredom and lovelessness. The age of fear seems to say, "Eat, drink, and be merry, because tomorrow we die!" But how merry can a man be with his mind obsessed by that fatal tomorrow?

Then, too, we are really not bad enough for undisguised self-worship. We have inherited two thousand years of Christian tradition; we have inherited, also, that innate moral sense of all mankind which makes even the most corrupt of us yearn vaguely for something better than himself to serve. And so we disguise the beast in the heart as a worthy cause; we borrow some shining virtue from heaven to robe it in, and make it into a false god. We proclaim that man will find salvation in art or science or education, in ending poverty or ending prejudice, in world government or in no government at all — everywhere but in the knowledge of the One.

They are hybrid creatures, our beast gods. Their strength comes from the true God, their weakness from disguised self-worship. Those which are most self-centered are easily rejected; any sane man can see that the alcoholic will not find salvation in the bottle or the nature boy in eating raw carrots and acquiring mosquito bites. But the really dangerous beasts are those cast in nobler shapes, with benevolent human masks on their faces. We call them by such names as human dignity, world peace, and freedom from want. And we revere them so deeply that we scream with horror when some iconoclast points out that at best they are means, not ends.

For of course such causes are good things — if we see them as angels, messengers of God, means by which we may come to know him, they are strong angels indeed. But if we make them our sole ends, they may easily become strong fiends. The ardent feminist who smashes her own home in the name of equal rights for women, the devoted pacifist who counsels submission to a Stalin and shuts his eyes to the bloodstains on his peace; the bureaucrat who in one country muzzles college professors in the name of free democracy and in another sends thousands to labor camps in the name of a Workers' Government — these are creatures for whom the angel has turned devil. What started, perhaps, as a genuine effort toward virtue has decayed into an excuse for self-righteousness and self-importance and personal power: a disguise for the beast in the heart.

Almost all of us, nowadays, are placing one or more of these false gods before God. The atheist gives himself wholly to his worthy cause, often achieving a burning singleness of purpose that makes him seem more religious than the religious; witness the whole-souled devotion for which the churches often envy the Communists. For the churchman is not capable of this evil simplicity. His heart is divided; he wants to worship both God *and* the beast. He speaks of God and country, God and prosperity, God and peace; forgetting, in the conscious nobility of his goal, that no man can serve two masters; forgetting, " Thou shalt have no other gods before me, *or in addition to me.*"

What thoughtful Protestant has not bewailed the lukewarmness of so much contemporary Protestantism? wondered over its halfhearted convictions, the limpness of its worship, its much chaff and little grain? A man trying to serve two masters is always halfhearted. We are torn by our conflicting loyalties; because we have not put God first and alone, we see no clear way before us in a crisis. When a man finds loyalty to God conflicting with loyalty to the Superstate, he is often incapable of deciding for himself at all. And the voice of God is a still, small voice at such times, whereas the beast god brays as loudly as the thunder.

Greatest among the false gods are these: Sex, the State, Science and Society.

Smiling at us from the billboard, the movie star proclaims: "Ah, sweet mystery of life, at last I've found you! Ah, at last I know the meaning of it all!" In the magazines the advertising captions clamor: Do as we say and you too shall know the meaning of it all! The insinuating voice on the radio whispers, "A woman's duty to herself . . ."

Openmouthed, the impressionable young drink it in, and proclaim that in love is their salvation. He who is not continually fizzing like champagne with sexual excitement is considered a failure in life. Nothing, no "outmoded morality" or promise or sense of obligation, must come between the worshiper and this supreme goal. The beast god has usurped the temple. And yet none of the false gods betrays his servant so quickly and obviously as the god Cupid; no pleasure vanishes so soon and leaves so much weariness and heartbreak behind. Sexuality can become a lasting joy only by becoming a sacrament in intention, a means to the service of God — a form through which men and women can feel for each other some slight prefiguring of the divine love. God comes first.

Hitler screams, "Kill the Jews!" and a legion of disciples springs to obey, bleating, "Orders is orders." Stalin proclaims, "All effort to combat the designs of imperialist warmongers!" and the young Communists fling themselves with fierce joy against Czech workers or Korean peasants. Meanwhile, what of the nominal Christians, the people who remember that God also has his law? Some of them die as martyrs. But many hang paralyzed with indecision, impotent with conflicting loyalties. On the one hand, the Lord is God; on the other hand, the State is God — how is a man to know? In the end, like the Pharisee in the parable of the Samaritan, they pass by on the other side of the road with averted faces. Who stood out against Hitler, who stood against Stalin, in those countries of the total State? Almost no one except the few Christians who knew that, even if a man must die for saying it — and how better can a Christian die? — God comes first. It remains to be seen if He will come before a Congressional committee!

"Science will find a way!" the professors tell us. Only ignorant and lazy men, they say, look to God for help; the intelligent modern can solve all his own problems, answer all his own questions, lift himself to an antiseptic heaven by his own bootstraps. "We can really begin to think of ourselves as responsible co-workers with God!" says the author of *Peace of Mind* naïvely. We no longer need an "outworn moral law"; all we need is a few more statistical surveys by a few more sociologists, and we shall be willing and able to get along with our neighbors. And yet all our sciences are no more than tools to increase our power of getting whatever we already want. They are an extension of what happened when the first savage made the first club. And unless the supreme authority of God tells us how to use our new tools, we shall use them exactly as the savage used the club — to beat out our neighbor's brains. Science will find a way — to make our cities huge blisters of radioactivity, to canker our countryside with new diseases carefully cultivated for their horror, to turn our planet into a white-hot globe of incandescent gas; unless we remember that God comes first.

What if a man be too temperate for sex worship, too just for State worship, too logical for Science worship? Is he free of the beasts? Alas, no; the subtlest of them all lies in wait for him. Nothing could seem more harmless, and indeed more Christian, than the adjuration, "Thou shalt serve the common good," given by one modern reviser of the Decalogue. "The safety of the people is the supreme law," was the way the ancient Romans put it. All things are just — if we do them for the good of society. Or, "It is expedient . . . that one man should die for the people."

So rapidly does "the common good," without God behind it, sink into a mere blown-up projection of each man's private desire! So readily does "the welfare of society" become a cloak for the seizure of power by an individual or a clique! The religion of Society has in our time become a well-organized worship, with its sociologist priests and its psychiatrist prophets. In that religion, "antisocial behavior" has been substituted for sin, and the "antisocial" man (i.e., the rebellious or merely unconventional man) is at once accused of "mental disturbance" — that is, of wrong thinking or what used to be called heresy. We lock up the heretic and torture him in ingenious ways with electric shocks and psychiatric third degrees, until he abjures his error and consents to serve the common good as *we* conceive it. And in all this we have the best intentions, as did the Spanish Inquisition. The "common good" may become a moloch to which countless individuals are sacrificed, if we forget that all good is in the love of God, and that God comes first.

There are other beast gods — as many as there are men to invent them. They wrangle in the temple, turning it into a den of thieves, deafening us with their conflicting counsel until we become incapable of acting effectively in any direction. In the end we cannot stay here; we shall choose one master or the other, and be saved or lost. But for the moment the choice is still before us. Let us remember that the complete backslider is always worse off than the man who never started to climb. The ancient polytheist was only a primitive, with a bright future of growth ahead of him. But the modern who whores after strange gods is a decadent, and there is nothing ahead of him but the dust and ashes of a burned-out world. Yet is was not to a primitive age that Christ came, but to one rotten with decay even beyond our own. Perhaps it is only the decadent — the man who has failed to live by the law, and who admits the measure of his failure — for whom the law will really prove a schoolmaster to bring him to Christ. Perhaps it is only the twentieth century self-worshiper who can learn the full meaning of the First Commandment.

Hold to this, and the beast in the heart has no power. The present loses its confusions, the future its terrors, and death itself is but the opening of a door.

" Thou shalt have no other gods before me."

That is the law of life and happiness and courage. Courage himself, God the Lion, stands beside us to help us live by it. Whatever we desire, whatever we love, whatever we find worth suffering for, will be Dead Sea fruit in our mouths unless we remember that God comes first.

II

GODS MADE WITH HANDS

Thou shalt not make unto thee any graven image, or any likeness of any thing that is in heaven above, or that is in the earth beneath, or that is in the water under the earth: thou shalt not bow down thyself to them, nor serve them: for I the Lord thy God am a jealous God, visiting the iniquity of the fathers upon the children unto the third and fourth generation of them that hate me; and showing mercy unto thousands of them that love me, and keep my commandments.
—Ex. 20:4–6.

WHAT SHAPE is an idol?

I worship Ganesa, brother, god of worldly wisdom, patron of shopkeepers. He is in the shape of a little fat man with an elephant's head; he is made of soapstone and has two small rubies for eyes. What shape do you worship?

I worship a fishtail Cadillac convertible, brother. All my days I give it offerings of oil and polish. Hours of my time are devoted to its ritual; and it brings me luck in all my undertakings; and it establishes me among my fellows as a success in life. What model is your car, brother?

I worship my house beautiful, sister. Long and loving meditation have I spent on it; the chairs contrast with the rug, the curtains harmonize with the woodwork, all of it is perfect and holy. The ash trays are in exactly the right place, and should some blasphemer drop ashes on the floor, I nearly die of shock. I live only for the service of my house, and it rewards me with the envy of my sisters, who must rise up and call me blessed. Lest my children profane the holiness of my house with dirt and noise, I drive them out of doors. What shape is your idol, sister? Is it your house, or your clothes, or perhaps even your worth-while and cultural club?

I worship the pictures I paint, brother. . . . I worship my job; I'm the best darn publicity expert this side Hollywood. . . . I worship my golf game, my bridge game. . . . I worship my comfort; after all, isn't enjoyment the goal of life? . . . I worship my church; I want to tell you, the work we've done in missions beats all other denominations in this city, and next year we can afford that new organ, and you won't find a better choir anywhere. . . . I worship myself. . . .

What shape is *your* idol?

The first carvers of idols were perhaps devout and innocent men. Anthropologists have a fashion of talking as if religion originated in mumbo jumbo, in blind fears and blind, unconscious desires; as if men set up elaborate rituals and made strange sacrifices without ever actually *thinking* about the nature of their gods.

Yet in all historic religions the metaphysics and philosophy have come first, the mumbo jumbo a late and corrupt second. Need we think worse of the men we have forgotten than of the men we remember? The inventors of idols must have had minds seething with the idea of God. Creator, Helper, Destroyer, he was all about them; the trees whispered and the animals cried aloud of him; the life-giving sun and death-dealing thunder spoke of the Most High. What was he like? How put him into words? They had no words: the language of savages is at best a clumsy tool, incapable of abstractions. But they had mind pictures and they had comparisons. His strength was as an elephant, his knowledge like the hawk's keen eye, his sudden anger like the crocodile striking unseen in the water. All these were forms of him and symbols of him. Musing, the savages felt that they knew what the Power was like; felt too the inexorable urge of all men to communicate their thoughts to others. They made an image of their thoughts.

So simply and innocently, perhaps, the idols may have begun; the elephant-headed, hawk-headed, crocodile-jawed grotesques, the man shapes with too many arms or too many teeth or even too much beauty to be merely mortal. There is no need to credit their inventors with a whole Freudian mythology of dark motives. Whatever their motives, this much is certain: the idol makers were trying to say what they thought about the nature of God. They were inventing what we call theology.

And we shall think less ill of idols if we remember that, after all, they were an advance upon the primitive creeds in which God was in all things equally and *was* essentially all things. To the idol maker God is one thing and not another; if he has the strength and wisdom of elephant or owl, he definitely does *not* have the weakness and silliness of mouse or jackdaw. However crude the concept, the human mind had to imagine a god who was elephant rather than mouse before it could understand a God who was good and not evil.

Unfortunately, the idols did not stay innocent long. There is an important distinction to be made between idol maker and idol worshiper. An old Hebrew legend declares that Abraham was once an idol maker, and that that was how he came to understand that idols are things made with hands and no true God. The idol maker may know, more or less clearly, that he is only giving shape to the half-formed concept of God in his head; that his images are solid metaphors — what we call symbols. The skeptical Greek philosopher may remind us that, after all, the image of Athena is only a symbol, only a means of fixing one's rambling thoughts upon the spirit that is Athena. Yet the idolater will persist in losing sight of the forest for the trees, and the god for the image. The gold and ivory statue of Athena becomes holy *in itself*, an answerer of prayer, a mysterious source of power, a material object somehow different from other objects. The crucifix, the plaster image, the saint's relic or miraculous medal or cheaply and illegibly printed Bible may become *themselves* things considered holy and magical, able to stop a bullet. Worse yet, the god confined in an image is a shrunken and powerless god.

Because you have limited your concept of God to a man shape on a carved crucifix, you may be in danger of inferring that you are free to outrage the man shapes walking and breathing around you. Because you worship the god in a specially baked wafer and a specially designed chalice, you may forget to worship the God of all bread and all wine. And yet it was said of the universal act of eating: "This do in remembrance of me."

Symbolism may thus be taken literally, so that the idol will rapidly beget mumbo jumbo. The mysterious Power, vast, formless, uncontrollable and unpredictable, which once filled the universe, is now for the idolater conveniently reduced to something he can imprison in a few ounces of wood or plaster. Do not think the idolater too foolish to know that his god is man-made and breakable. He does know it; that is precisely the sort of god he wants — a god he can control.

The essence of idolatry is its attempt to control and enslave the deity. If the idol has power over man, so has man power over the idol; he can bribe it, he can drive a bargain with it, by certain rituals and sacrifices he can compel it to grant his wishes. Or so, at least, the idolater thinks. For an idol is not just an image, of one shape or another, meant to represent a deity. An idol is a material object, by the proper manipulation of which a man may get what he wants out of life.

Only, of course, he can't. The universe is not made that way; there is no such power in any material object. Sacrifice as much as you please, cajole and flatter as you please, beat your disobedient idol with a big stick if you please — the thing still won't give you what you want. In consequence, all idolatrous cultures tend to get nastier and nastier. If a small bribe doesn't succeed, men raise the ante; they offer more. The idol will not respond to a dance of virgins with flowers? Very well, let's try a dance of warriors mutilating themselves with knives. You have cut off a lock of your hair and laid it before the idol, yet life is still dark? Try cutting your first-born's throat and offering *him*. Nor does the idol's continued silence teach you better sense, if you're a natural-born idolater.

For if Mumbo Jumbo is so hard to please, what a very great Mumbo Jumbo he must be!

All Mesopotamia wallowed in this nastiness when the Hebrews, first of history's iconoclasts, rose up and said, "Thou shalt make unto thyself no graven images."

They were thorough, those Hebrews. Since images could be so misused, they would have no images at all — not for the most innocent purposes. No chryselephantine statue in the Temple, no gnarled wooden lumps of household gods in the home; no, not so much as an animal head to ornament an armchair or a bird shape woven into a rug. By the time of Christ the Roman eagles, which were essentially what a flag is today, were regarded as an abomination which could not be admitted into any Jewish city. In the end even making a *mental* image of God was prohibited.

How effective was the Commandment? It was very effective in one way: it completely destroyed the graphic arts of the Jews. Solomon's Temple was splendid with cherubim and golden bulls; yet for the last two thousand years the Jews who have accomplished so much with music and literature have done almost nothing with sculpture and painting. In the same way the Mohammedan world, which borrowed the prohibition of images, was compelled to limit its art to the intricate and formalized doodles we term "arabesques." But as for destroying idolatry itself . . .

What shape is an idol?

Need it be a man shape or a beast shape? May it not be any possible shape men can devise — anything from a dynamo to a mink coat — as long as you look to it for your salvation? The rigid Hebrew rule kept you from ornamenting your furniture, but it never kept you from worshiping your furniture. As well try to rescue a man from slavish devotion to his automobile by removing the doodad on its radiator cap!

An idol is worshiped, not for its shape, but for its imagined power. The scribes and Pharisees did not succeed in stopping idolatry; they only changed its vocabulary. Instead of asking a man shape for help, we now "look for the salvation of

society to the proper harnessing of the forces of the atom."
There are still some who kneel before images, making small
offerings and promising big ones, begging for their heart's
desire and watching the painted plaster face for miraculous
smiles or tears. But most of us modern Christian idolaters
worship gadgets instead of images. We will be happy if only
we can buy the new television set or the new patent garbage
disposer. Lenin thought the salvation of Russia lay in electric
power; Americans, having tried the dynamo in vain, now look
further — to the mysterious powers of the cyclotron. The
greatest idol of our time has the shape of a mushroom cloud.

Does it matter which of our toys we make into a god? What
matters is that the thing is still a toy, an idol — a material
object on which we rely to bring us happiness. Idolatry's
other name is materialism. As long as we hope to be saved by
the work of our own hands, we remain idolaters and the Second Commandment applies to us literally. What shape has
your idol, brother? It may be quite primitive still — a rabbit's
foot set in a cheap brass mounting. Or it may be subtle and
civilized — a radiation perceptible only to the electron micro-
scope. Whatever men have made, that they may worship;
there are men who worship modern plumbing and hope to
redeem China and India with the flush toilet.

All sins, theologians tell us, are entering wedges for the
great and ultimate sin of self-worship. Why should I prefer
to worship a small and limited idol, rather than a great and
universal God? Perhaps because I can *own* the idol, whereas
no man can own God, whose justice is incorruptible. Tom's
elephant godling is supposed to answer Tom's prayers, not
Dick's; and Dick's snake fetish is expected to protect Dick
against Harry. The great and universal God, however, loves
all men alike — how, then, dare I ask him to help me to get
the better of my competitors? But my fishtail Cadillac con-
fers glory upon me alone, not on the lesser breeds without
Cadillacs. Mrs. Jones's perfectly appointed house gratifies
Mrs. Jones precisely because Mrs. Robinson, who lives next
door, hasn't got it.

The tragedy is that we really know better. We *know* happiness is a spiritual state, not to be achieved by piling up wealth or seizing power. For two thousand years we have been listening to preachers tell us that; and we have never failed to nod our heads in agreement. Nowadays our psychologists and even many of our popular novelists are repeating the same lesson. We buy their inspirational books by the ten thousand, we condemn materialism every hour on the hour, we denounce with horror that rigidly organized idolatry called Communism, with its doctrine that by the work of your factories you shall be saved. Daily the revival of religion gains new strength — only by a return to Christianity, we proclaim, can we save the things we most value in life. Of course we know better than to worship idols!

If only men could live up to what they know! But men, Saint Paul said, are creatures corrupted by original sin, living by the law in their members rather than the law of their minds; creatures who obey emotion and appetite and habit far more often than they obey knowledge. In the very act of appealing to Christ, we relapse into our habitual idolatry. We must return to Christianity, yes; but why? Because it is true? But do we, in our hearts, believe that it is true, that Christ is the Son of God and that we must follow him even at the cost of renouncing *this* life and all its treasures? We say little about that, much about our need for Christianity to protect our treasures. Yet surely Christianity was not meant to save the world for us; it was meant to save us from the world.

Unlike Buddhists and Hindus, Christians have usually held that the good things of this life are good indeed, that all enjoyment is a foreshadowing of our ultimate enjoyment of God. Our earthly loves and joys are meant to lead us to Christ, and we may certainly ask the Christ in whom we believe to preserve them for us. Yet this is very different from *using* Christ without believing in him — from making Christian doctrine into a propaganda weapon, a pep talk to hearten us to go out and fight for good old materialism. We must return to Christianity in order to preserve the things we value — but we cannot return to Christianity at all unless the thing we value above all else is Christ. If we are reviving religion only in order to defend our own works, from the American Constitution down to the famous American blueberry pie, we are in effect asking Christ to save our idols for us.

Thus we can't automatically shed our idolatry just by going to church. Certainly we will progress to a better grade of idolatry, as it were; the church will make us ashamed of our grosser and more selfish idols. I began, perhaps, by wanting a television set in my own living room to impress the neighbors. After a year of churchgoing, behold me out raising money to buy a television set for the teen-agers' clubhouse! I have come a long way. A self-centered materialist has become an unselfish, public-spirited pillar of the church. Yet, though I have been cured of trying to save myself by gadgets, I still think the community can be saved by them.

Another year, and I may have got past this social-services view of religion. It has dawned upon me that the church is more than a convenient tool for community reform; I see it now as something unique and desirable in its own right, something of which better housing and better child care and better citizenship and better government are the by-products and not the goals. What I want *now* is to build the church itself.

And I am still an idolater. I have fallen into the last and subtlest trap; I bow down to wood and stone, in the shape of a church building. Through regular attendance, through handsome financial contributions, through raising the minister's salary and redecorating the altar and improving the organist's technique and encouraging the foreign missions, I expect to be saved. To put it bluntly, I have forgotten that the church itself is not God.

So easy to confuse the means with the end! And yet, if the church is anything except a means to the knowledge of God, the church is nothing but a bore. (Perhaps that's why it so often *is* a bore.) When the church becomes an idol, a thing mysteriously holy and powerful in itself, then the goal of

religion becomes getting people to church — no matter why
they go or what they get out of it. Rope them in with a Bingo
game or a lecture on Freudian psychiatry, it's all one; the act
of crossing the threshold has the magical power of saving
them.

Christianity has never been quite free from this particular
form of idolatry — what some have called "churchianity."
The seventeenth century Puritans saw that a beautiful church
and a beautiful ritual could easily become idols, and hoped
to avoid the danger by making ritual and church as bare and
ugly as they could. But almost at once there arose new Baalim:
church organization, church discipline, or even the Bible itself, read assiduously morning and night and seldom understood at all. Men thought they were bringing their children to
Christ by forcing them to sit still, white and frightened, listening to the edifying tale of how Joshua slaughtered babies or
Elisha sent she-bears to eat up bad little boys.

Today we are especially tempted to worship of the church
because we often have nothing left to worship *except* the
church. In our eagerness to end the old vain feuds between
creeds, many of us have adopted a "modernist" Christianity
with practically no creed at all; in our desire to escape religious prejudice, we have proclaimed that the important
thing is to have a place of worship, no matter what sort of
something you worship when you get there. With such an attitude, the church becomes an idol by default. At this moment
there are spiritualists in our cities whose "divine services"
consist of sham mind reading done by sleight of hand — and
their congregations accept them as Christian ministers.

Very well then! we are all idolaters still. But why not?
After all, our best thoughts about God are only metaphors,
verbal and mental idols; we speak of God as a spirit, without
body, parts, or passions, yet we cannot conceive a spirit
without inventing some sort of form and substance for it.
Granted that most idols are crude and silly metaphors indeed,
still a man can learn only from his mistakes, and sooner or
later we'll progress to better metaphors. Meanwhile, we may

reason, we're worshiping the best thing we know, and though the gadget is not God, neither is it the devil. An idol is only an inanimate object that can do no harm. . . .

So is a gun. But a man can do great harm with it.

Idolatry lies not in the idol but in the worshiper. It is a psychological attitude that governs his whole life, and a very murderous attitude. We begin by offering others to the idol; we end by offering ourselves. Men threw their babies into the fiery furnace of Moloch and threw themselves before the crushing car of Jagannath; men unconsciously sacrifice themselves and their children daily to the automobile juggernaut and the brain-consuming furnace of the modern city. The house devours the housewife, the office rots the executive with ulcers, the canned entertainments leave us incapable of entertaining ourselves. We feel that if bombs ever destroy our elaborate gadget prison it will mean " the end of civilization " — yet not so long ago Americans faced a wilderness with nothing but their two hands, a long rifle, and an ax. Have our idols done us no harm?

The real horror of idols is not merely that they give us nothing, but that they take away from us even that which we have. By the act of imagining power in the fetish we rob ourselves, and the Holy Spirit within us, of that much power. If only our automobile can rush us away from danger, we have lost the power of saving ourselves by our legs. An idolater is always a spiritual paralytic. The more we look to material objects for help, the less we can help ourselves or ask help from the grace of God. If we are to be saved, it will not be by wood, however well carved and polished; nor by machines, however efficient; nor by social planning, however ingenious. If we are to be saved, it must be by the one power that is built into a man at his beginning and that he does not have to make with his hands — the power of the Holy Spirit, which is God.

III

THE WORD WAS WITH GOD

*Thou shalt not take the name of the Lord thy God in vain:
for the Lord will not hold him guiltless that taketh his name in
vain.*

—Ex. 20:7.

THE CORPSE-FAT CANDLES burn blue. The thing that lies bound
on the black altar struggles and whimpers faintly. Within
his mystic pentacle the dark priest stands, eyes burning under
his hood, intoning the sinister invocation of his creed, the
reversed Lord's Prayer. Deeper in the shadows of the velvet-
hung room, the huddled worshipers echo his words in harsh
whispers.

"Heaven in art who Father our . . ."

The air in the room is drowsy with drugged incense; the
shadows seem coming alive, quivering with power. The priest
raises his knife, chanting the magical names of God.

"Aglon Tetragram Vaycheon Retragsammathon Eryona
Onera El Eloe Zelioz Ramathel Shaddai Elohim . . ."

The knife descends. The worshipers breathe raggedly in
horrid expectation.

"Messias Soter Emmanuel Sabaoth Adonai . . ."

The sacrifice on the altar stares up with wide, terrified eyes.

The priest speaks the ultimate magical name, that which
sums up in itself the seventy-two divine names of power.

"Shemhamphorash!" he cries, and cuts the throat of the
bound child on the altar.

Incredible than anyone should so misuse the name of God?
Yet it has happened: two thousand years ago in Judea and
Rome and Egypt, two-hundred-odd years ago in France at

the court of His Most Christian Majesty Louis XIV, and even today in dark corners of great cities and dark backwoods farms. Belief in the magical powers of names dies hard — witness the present popularity of numerologists, who will turn your name into numbers for you in the approved style of the medieval Kabbala and will tell you whether the result is propitious or unpropitious. Witness too the advertisers' successful trick of selling you their most doubtful wares — anything from toothpaste and diet fads to theories of psychology or government — by labeling them with the great and magical name of Science.

We can only guess how the belief in word magic began, for it is as old as language. The savage called his friend's name, and saw his friend turn and answer; what more natural to conclude than that the name itself in some way *compelled* an answer? Just so did Adam in the Garden name all the beasts and thus establish himself as their master. At the beginning of history we find men thinking that possession of the real name of anything — man, beast, city, or God — gave them power over the thing itself. The city of Rome had a " real " name, kept secret by the priests lest an enemy learn it and use it for hostile magic; kept secret so successfully that we do not know it to this day. The God of the Hebrews had a " real " name, too full of power for men to write it or speak it; for a while only the high priest was allowed to invoke it, once a year, in the privacy of the Holy of Holies. Eventually even he dared not utter the sacred syllables, and so the Name is lost to us — scholars have spent fruitless years trying to reconstruct it.

And we can only guess, likewise, at the end of word magic; for the end is not yet. At this moment there are men solemnly discussing whether their government is a " real " democracy. There are literary critics writing whole books to prove that someone they dislike isn't " really " a poet, psychologists attacking an opponent by arguing that his theory isn't " really " scientific, biologists tearing their hair trying to decide whether an almost indetectable microorganism is " really " a plant or an animal, doctors inspiring awe by assuring patients that their bellyaches are " really " gastritis (the Greek word for bellyache) or their cracked wits " really " schizophrenia (the Greek word for cracked wits). None of these learned labels tell us anything about the object and its nature; they are concerned only with vague shades of definition in the arguer's mind. And behind all such gobbledygook lurks the mind of the simple savage, imagining that by naming a thing he acquires power over it. To students of language, words are no more than the arbitrary, crude, and at best inadequate, labels we attach to things for our own convenience. But to believers in word magic the label *is* the thing, and a rose by any other name doesn't smell like a rose.

The more powerful the object, therefore, the more powerful its name must be; and what is so powerful as the dread name of God? " Thou shalt not take it in vain," is a misleading phrase to modern ears, for the original point was that one *couldn't* take it in vain, in our sense. That is, if one called on God by his right name, however casually, things started to happen! Clay figures came to life, enemies withered away, an aging mistress recaptured King Louis' love. Even Satanists, calling up the devil, use the name of God to control him; the Black Mass must be celebrated by a duly ordained priest with a properly consecrated wafer. Jews of the eighth century B.C. thought that the Name would bring down fire from the sky. Jews of the Middle Ages wrote in the Sepher Hasidim, the Book of the Pious:

" One may not say that the invocation of God's name obliges him to do the will of the invoker, that God himself is coerced by the recital of his name; but the Name itself is invested with the power to fulfill the desire of the man who utters it."

And do not many contemporary Christians feel that using the Name casually in conversation is in some way an insult to God?

Thus the Third Commandment is not just a nice-Nellyish warning against profanity. It is much more like the sort of warning you see around power plants: "Danger — High Voltage!" For the ancient Hebrews seem to have thought of God almost literally as a live wire. II Samuel, ch. 6, relates how Uzzah, who touched the Ark unwarily while trying to keep it from falling, was struck dead by the indwelling Power. The implied moral seems to be: Be careful how you touch God — he's dangerous!

Where there is power, however, men will try to use it for their own ends, good and bad. For a long while Jehovah was not conceived as either good or bad; he was only Force — the lightnings playing about the cloudy head of Sinai. And just as today we employ the force of atomic fission alike to kill or cure, so men used Jehovah. Father cursing fractious children, priest hoping to cure a leper, desert raider lusting for the wealth of an unsuspecting city — they called upon the Name, and the Name, they thought, obeyed. Few enterprises were too black or too bloody for its help.

Then the Third Commandment came crashing down on the heads of the black magicians. The Lord was a Lord of righteousness; he was not to be invoked for evil ends.

Whether this realization came gradually or suddenly, it was new and devastating. For what was prohibited was the misuse of power. Modern churches try to prohibit this also; but, let us admit it, with little hope of success in a materialist world. Yet the ancient Hebrews, God-inspired, tried and up to a point succeeded.

Up to a point only; their literalness defeated them. If the Name were the only source of power that God had given us tabooing the Name might well prevent power from bein misused. Yet even then there were other power sources. There was the State, for instance, by means of which Ahab stole Naboth's vineyard and some modern Governments tax their small businessmen out of existence or herd their peasants into collective farms. There was the sword; there was money. And, among shaven-headed Egyptian priests or bearded, disputatious Greek philosophers, there were the first stirrings of a new and terrible magic — the manipulation of the power of God inherent in matter, the manipulation that we call Science.

As time wore on, indeed, these powers of man took precedence over the power of God. In Christ's day, though the original Name was still mystically taboo, new names of God were accepted as perfectly harmless; the rose by another name had ceased to be a rose. Men called upon Jehovah constantly to witness that they'd be beggared if they paid one shekel more for that camel load of spices — called upon him by all manner of indirect Oriental epithets, such as Him-Up-There, The Old One, and You-Know-Who. "God strike me dead if I'm lying!" they said, and lied. The misuse of power had given place to the contempt of power. It was of this sort of swearing, with its implied disbelief in the God of righteousness, that Christ warned: "Swear not at all."

Today, with two thousand years of additional practice, we have invented many new ways of breaking the Third Commandment. We still misuse God's power and we still despise it; we call upon God to justify our sins; we commit the ultimate blasphemy of not calling upon God at all. Many churchgoers think of the Third Commandment as meant primarily to forbid casual profanity. Yet casual profanity is perhaps the least of our offenses against it.

It is true that we often speak of God too lightly, making an empty noise out of the most real and profound of human experiences, substituting a meaningless verbal habit for a serious concept of the Almighty. Profanity does not insult God — a man cannot insult God; but it does cripple man. Significantly enough, no one swears by God so readily as the professed atheist.

The mealymouthed among us have confused the issue by extending their notion of profanity to cover anything that frightens them — and what does not frighten them? They dare not speak irreverently of the devil, whom God forbid that we should reverence; they dare not call bodily functions by their right Anglo-Saxon names. Until recently the word "syphilis" was unprintable, and today there are still some

magazines that think twice before printing the word " cancer."
Among the mealymouthed, the objection to swearing is mainly
that, " It's so unrefined! " Their whole psychology was neatly
summed up in an advertising slogan of a few years back: " Spit
is a horrid word! "

Perhaps the objection to plain Anglo-Saxon is partly an
unlucky hang-over from the days when Latin was the language of educated men, and only the common herd spoke
" the vulgar tongue." Modern English retains a double vocabulary, with polysyllabic Latin and Greek synonyms for most
of its blunt, short words, and those who shudder at " spit "
and " sweat " have no objection to " expectorate " and " per-
spire." Here belief in word magic persists in its most ridiculous
form, as if an offensive subject could be covered by a per-
fumed label! But how disastrous a refinement it is that classes
the name of God in such a sense among the unspeakables!

The casually profane, however, are seldom guilty of anything worse than carelessness and light-mindedness. What
about the misusers of power, the black magicians?

Dark corners of cities, dark backwoods farms; but nowhere
else, surely? Only the most primitive Pennsylvania hexerei,
the most degenerate Hollywood occultism, calls upon the
name of Power for such purposes nowadays. The rest of us
have long since ceased to conjure with the power of the
Name, for the very good reason that we don't believe the
Name has any.

Yet if the Commandment was meant to forbid the misuse of
power, we have our own ways of breaking it. The ancient
Hebrews, inexperienced in science, thought power lay in the
pronunciation of certain syllables. Modern man knows better.
" I cannot," says Goethe's Faust, translating The Gospel According to St. John, " I cannot value the Word so highly . . .
I shall write *In the beginning was the Fact*."

We of the twentieth century are aware that the power of
God is expressed primarily in his works, not in a name men
have invented for him. The question to be asked of us, then,
is what use we have made of his works.

A very effective use, judging by the newspapers. Our biologists have bred germs that could poison our enemies. Our chemists have developed gases that could choke our enemies. Our physicists have triumphantly split the unsplittable, and thereby annihilated our enemies. Our psychologists have learned how to enslave our enemies' minds — and our own.

What judgment shall be passed upon us, if the true meaning of the prohibition is: Thou shalt not use the power of God for evil ends? Wherever science has given one man control of another man, science has broken the Third Commandment.

Nor can we limit ourselves to condemning the sins of the outer world. We of the churches often gather our robes away from contamination, and thank God that we are not as other men. We don't despise God's name; in fact, we call upon it constantly to justify ourselves. How few parents, annoyed past bearing by a young child, can resist the facile, "God will punish you!" How few strait-laced churchwomen, outraged by the shamelessness (and popularity) of the town's bad girl, can keep from secret satisfaction at the thought of the divine judgment awaiting her! If we object to meat-eating, we declare that God is vegetarian; if we abhor war, we proclaim a pacifist Deity. He who turned water into wine to gladden a wedding is now accused by many of favoring that abominable fluid grape juice.

There can hardly be a more evil way of taking God's name in vain than this way of presuming to speak in it. For here is spiritual pride, the ultimate sin, in action — the sin of believing in one's own righteousness. The true prophet says humbly, "To me, a sinful man, God spoke." But the scribes and Pharisees declare, "When we speak, God agrees." They feel no need of a special revelation, for they are always, in their own view, infallible. It is this self-righteousness of the pious that most breeds atheism, by inspiring all decent ordinary men with loathing of the enormous lie.

Nor is Pharisaism confined to individuals. Whole nations practice it; many a campaign of looting has been proclaimed as a holy war. And whole churches, indeed all the churches, have fallen victim to it at one time or another; from the pathetic backwoods sect of hysterics to the pomp and majesty of Rome, all have at one time or another claimed to hold a monopoly in God. The Protestants who are at times overeager to see the mote in the Roman Catholic eye might do well to look up their own ecclesiastical history; they will find there such things as the seventeenth century Kirk of Scotland calling for the massacre of women and children in God's name.

"Many will say to me in that day, Lord, Lord. . . . And then will I profess unto them, I never knew you: depart from me, ye that work iniquity." There has only been One who always spoke for God.

One stranger way of misusing the name of God is the modern trick of not using it at all. Many, though their hearts may ache for a faith, have so many painful associations connected with the very *word* "God" that they cannot bear the sound of it. The too stern father, the too fatuous Sunday school teacher, the too simpering religious picture, the too dull sermon — all have combined to give the divine name overtones of boredom, disgust, and disbelief. "One word is too often profaned for me to profane it!" some moderns might say, as Shelley said of the word "love." And so they substitute for the Name all manner of evasive phrases — First Cause, Life Force, Cosmic Oversoul, Universal Law. A dangerous attraction of such phrases is that Causes and Forces and the like aren't gods of *justice* — they may have made you, but once that's done, they forget all about you and don't keep tabs on your little habits. Usually, however, the reason for believing in a Life Force rather than a God is less sinful than silly. Question a Force enthusiast, and ten to one he will say, "I can't believe in a God — an old man with white whiskers sitting on a cloud!" As if any Christian above the level of infant or imbecile ever did believe in a God of that sort!

Here we have a new type of word magic — the Name, once tabooed because it was so great, is now tabooed because it is so small. As C. S. Lewis points out, those who think to make their concept of God larger by talking of Ultimate Principles and such are in reality only making it vaguer; they are reducing the good, wise, and loving Being to an abstraction incapable of goodness, wisdom, or love — and indeed of being too! Offhand it would seem as if there were no harm in a man's inventing his own name for the Almighty, yet in practice rejecting the word almost always leads to rejecting the reality. For words do have one sort of magic — they have a magical power over the operations of our thinking. When we drop the word "God," we are on the way to losing touch with the truth behind it. There is no virtue in not calling upon Him on the ground that he isn't there to answer.

Thus a necessary corollary of the Third Commandment must be: Thou shalt take the name of the Lord thy God in earnest! We who have used the Name for unhallowed ends, from necromancy down to getting our own way in a family quarrel; we who have misused the power God put in flesh and coal, in wood and waterfalls, in solid matter and in empty space; we who have called upon God to bolster up our own vanity, or have *not* called upon him for the sake of soothing our prejudice — we are all black magicians, and, like Elymas the sorcerer, we have been struck blind for our sins and now grope in mist and darkness. Habitually, day after day, we have taken God's name in vain. Let us, if we can, teach ourselves to take it in earnest. It is high time.

IV

DAY OF REJOICING

Remember the sabbath day, to keep it holy. Six days shalt thou labor, and do all thy work: but the seventh day is the sabbath of the Lord thy God: in it thou shalt not do any work, thou, nor thy son, nor thy daughter, thy manservant, nor thy maidservant, nor thy cattle, nor thy stranger that is within thy gates: for in six days the Lord made heaven and earth, the sea, and all that in them is, and rested the seventh day: wherefore the Lord blessed the sabbath day, and hallowed it.

— Ex. 20:8–11.

THE MARTIAN STUDENT, swooping dangerously low over these United States in his flying saucer, scribbled furiously with his writing tentacle. He had chosen an ideal morning for taking notes — a fine summer Sunday, with all the natives coming out of their houses and obligingly spreading themselves around for his observation. But he was in a desperate hurry. Only one more week till his thesis was due, and without it he hadn't an earthman's chance of passing his comparative anthropology course.

As it turned out, though, he needn't have worried. The report he wrote was brilliant, comparing favorably for accuracy and insight with the best work of our earthly anthropologists. In several Martian colleges professors have read it aloud as a shining example of what modern scientific methods can do.

"Like so many primitive life forms [thus went the Martian's report] the creatures of the third planet are sun worshipers. One day in every seven is set apart for the adoration of their deity, weather permitting. Their rituals vary, and each apparently involves a special form of dress; but all are conducted in the open air, and most seem to require the collec-

tion of enormous crowds. Some creatures gather in vast
arenas, to watch strangely garbed priests perform elaborate
ceremonies involving a ball and variously shaped instruments
of wood. (The significance of the ball as a solar symbol, of
course, is known to every Martian schoolboy.) Others, no
doubt the mystics and solitaries of their religion, prefer to
address the ball themselves with long clubs, singly or in
groups of two or four, wandering in green fields. Some,
stripping themselves almost naked in their ecstasy, go down
to the seashore in great throngs and there perform their rites,
often hurling themselves into the waves with frenzied cries.
(This practice is unmistakably based on the dogma, found
also among the semi-intelligent crustaceans of Venus, that the
sun is a sea-god born anew each morning from the ocean; the
use of large brightly colored balls in these seaside rituals is
confirmatory evidence.) After the ceremonial immersion, devotees have been observed to anoint themselves with holy
oils and stretch themselves out full length with eyes closed,
in order to surrender themselves entirely to silent communion
with the deity.

" Human sacrifice, sad to say, is also practiced, the instru-
ment of death being a four-wheeled metal car which may be
employed in various ways. Often a chosen victim is run down
and crushed. Even more frequently the sacrifice is voluntary;
devotees enter the cars, and either work themselves into a
frenzy by traveling at high speed until they dash themselves
to bits against other cars or stationary objects — or else con-
gregate in vast throngs, too closely packed to move, and allow
the sun's rays beating upon the hot metal to cook them slowly
to death.

" There exists, however, a small sect of recalcitrants or heretics that does not practice sun worship. These may be identi-
fied by their habit of clothing themselves more soberly and
completely than the sun worshipers. They too gather in
groups, but only to hide from the sun in certain buildings of
doubtful use, usually with windows of glass colored to keep
out the light. It is not clear whether these creatures are simply

unbelievers or whether they are excommunicated from sun worship for some offense — we have not been able to discover what goes on within their buildings, which may perhaps be places of punishment. But it is noteworthy that their faces and gestures show none of the almost orgiastic religious frenzy with which the sun worshipers pursue their devotions. In fact, they usually appear relaxed and even placid, thus indicating minds blank of thought or emotion; in this connection, see Dr. Duerf's monumental study, *Totem and Taboo Among the Giant Centipedes of Mercury*."

Was the Martian wildly wrong, or fantastically right?

Sunday is still a holiday to all of us, but for many it has long since ceased to be a holy day. Violation of the Sabbath is one of the great sorrows of the modern churchman. Half the churches are empty, while all the popular places of entertainment are crowded. True, men seldom work on the Sabbath if they can help it; but how passionately, how unscrupulously, they play on it! Nor can we force them to stop playing. Our old blue laws have rightly fallen into disuse; they were an outrage against the conscience of a country built on the Christian religion and on its inescapable corollary, the principle of religious freedom. When a man contemplates forcing his own convictions down another man's throat, he is contemplating both an unchristian act and an act of treason to the United States.

So the unbelievers must go on with their games. But what of the believers? It is so easy for them to be tempted into joining the games, first now and then, later as a habit; finally, the uneasy sense of something forgotten on Sunday morning gradually fades away entirely, and faith in God perishes not by conviction but by disuse. Even many who do come to church come out of a dull sense of duty rather than a joyous sense of devotion — the life has gone out of their belief. Others, instead of stirring their stumps, listen in comfortable living rooms to a sermon on the radio, arguing that it is "just the same." They have forgotten that one of the first necessities of the Christian life is a congregation, a physical coming together; that the communion is between man and man as well as between man and God; that solitary worship, except for some few specially called to the ascetic life, is hardly Christian worship at all.

And it is no use scolding them. In the end, a man will love a scolding church no better than a nagging wife, and may very well desert both. Nor is it much use begging them — saying, in effect, "We know we're a horrible bore and the golf course is much more fun; still, sacrifice yourselves to us for conscience' sake!" For the whole essence of a church is that it must *not* be a horrible bore; it must be love and beauty and delight beyond all other delights, if it is truly to exist in His name. Otherwise it must fail and dwindle into a dead formality, and no threats or pleadings will give it much semblance of life.

How does one keep a day holy? By making it unpleasant, and restrictive, and boring — or by making it joyous? By making it as much as possible like hell, or as much as possible like heaven?

There are two texts in the Bible that may hint at an answer, one in the Old Testament: "God saw every thing that he had made, and, behold, it was very good," and one in the New: "The sabbath was made for man, and not man for the sabbath."

One cannot escape the conviction that certain elements in the churches have themselves unintentionally done much to make the Sabbath unholy. It took the strict Puritans of England only ten years — from 1650 to 1660 — so to disgust the people with legislated piety that they reacted into a license undreamed of before. Perhaps the willful license of our own Sundays originated partly in a kind of bravado, a resentment of legislated controls and negative virtues. When bigots interpreted the Fourth Commandment to mean *Thou shalt not enjoy life on Sunday,* did not all pandemonium raise a howl of triumph? The Puritan tradition has given America great things — education and freedom and a concept of ethics in government; yet, alas, for many people today the name "Puritan" has become a scoffing and a byword, synonymous with kill-joy. Not that the Puritans were really foes to *all* joy. But they did think a purely intellectual and spiritual concentration on God was the only religious experience worth seeking. They did smash stained-glass windows in Old England, and frown on children at play in New England — see their school advertisements. And, like all who lack charity, they preferred negative methods; they believed you could make people enjoy God by forbidding them to enjoy anything else.

Question a dozen modern infidels about their childhood, and half of them will trace their atheism to endless dull, bleak Sundays in a negatively "Christian" household which made a child's life seem hardly worth living. The ball games, the dances, the speeding automobiles, the crowded beaches of today's Sabbath — they are fugitive and inadequate pleasures, no doubt. Yet for many they may be an attempt, however fumbling, to restore to the Sabbath some of that holy gladness which it had before overzealous reformers turned the Fourth Commandment's "thou shalt" into a "thou shalt not."

Cast back into history, and the true meaning of the Sabbath is easy enough to find. "Thou shalt not do any *work*, thou, nor thy son, nor thy daughter, thy manservant, nor thy maidservant, nor thy cattle, nor thy stranger that is within thy gates." On this one day, man returned to Eden. The curse of Adam was lifted, the primal Fall undone somewhat, and all creatures caught a glimmering of the paradisal state in which everything God had made was very good. On this one day a man was commanded to enjoy himself.

In the early years of Israel, men celebrated the Sabbath as a feast, in just this spirit. With the rise of an organized and legalistic priesthood, however, the day of gladness and rejoicing soon gave way to a day of discipline. The prohibition of work was interpreted with an awful literalness; one might not light a fire, cook a dinner, or use one's false teeth. In Christ's time, there were 1,521 things one could *not* do on the Sabbath — including rescuing a drowning man. Until

the resolute Maccabees taught them better, Jewish armies
would let themselves be slaughtered on the Sabbath rather
than perform the "work" of self-defense. The fire taboo,
among others, is still in force; orthodox Jews may neither
kindle nor quench a flame on Saturday. A group of them recently stoned a fire engine in Jerusalem for putting out a fire
on the Sabbath. And in New York's East Side the "shabbas
goy" is a traditional institution — the Sabbath Gentile, usually
a needy drunk or an underfed child, who earns a few cents by
turning on the Jewish stoves which the pious, bound by letter
rather than spirit, dare not light for themselves.

Absurd? But remember that the distinction between act
and intention, letter and spirit, hardly existed at all before
Christ made it for us; nor can it be preserved without the
constant guidance of Christ. The modern world makes it im-
perfectly, the ancient world seldom dreamed of it. In the
old days, work was work and sin was sin. Was picking an
apple work, by ordinary definition? Then work it remained,
though you did it in sheer playfulness. Did killing a man make
you guilty of blood? Then you were bloodguilty even if he
killed himself purposely by throwing himself before your
chariot. Thus Oedipus in the Greek play must bear the full
shame of parricide and incest, though it is by a quite innocent
mistake that he has killed his father and married his mother.
And thus the Pharisees rebuked Jesus for Sabbath-breaking
when he healed the sick. The answer was a flash of that divine
common sense of which the human race is commonly incapable — "The sabbath was made for man, and not man for the
sabbath."

The words shattered, for a time, the whole iron prison of
prohibitions which had turned a day of joy and love into a
day of sullenness and fear. The Christian Sabbath was a feast
indeed — the love feast, the communal meal of worship. No
one thought of it as the renunciation of pleasure; it was every
man's pleasure and supreme delight. The ancient Romans,
their own religion long since dwindled to spiritless and skeptical routine, suspected the Christians of perpetrating obscene

orgies on their Sabbath—on the ground that Christians obviously enjoyed the Sabbath so much!

On this groundwork of joy the medieval church built the
great festivals of the Christian Year. Not for those days the
modern distinction between the religious and the secular;
they had grasped the truth that all of life is holy. The earth
turned round its eternal wheel in heaven, the seasons changed.
Midwinter brought the birth of the new year and the birth
of God; after a season of darkness spring came with the
resurrection of Christ among the reborn flowers. And all glad
things of the seasons—flower and fruit, the stars in their
courses and the pleasant doings of men—all testified to the
Glory. A house was built, a child begotten, a bridge thrown
across an abyss, a cathedral aimed at the sky—in God's name,
every one. A multitude danced in the streets, or paraded in
beautiful and fantastic costumes, or sang songs, or put on
amateur theatricals—and God was the theme of dance and
song and parade and play. Of course men fell short; of course,
day after day, the Middle Ages slipped back into the usual
human cruelties and lusts, greeds and fears. Yet still they
believed. To them there was no such thing as a secular matter,
a part of man's life that wasn't God's business. A man could
not so much as put on his shoes of a morning without God
helping him to tie the laces aright, and the devil trying to
muddle his fingers and make him lose his temper. Medieval
thought reached its height in the feast of Corpus Christi—
the festival of the body of the man Jesus, the celebration of
the Word made flesh, the solemn affirmation that this life, for
all its corruptions and betrayals, is nevertheless the work of
God—twisted by Satan, yes, but never altogether stripped of
glory, and in the end redeemed into the eternal splendor
of heaven. Out of this view of life grew the Christian Sabbath,
in which man, like God, rested from his labors and saw that
the world was good.

Unfortunately, man cannot for long endure the common
sense of God.

Side by side with Christianity, and often mistaken for it,

there has always existed a dark Eastern religion of despair. Perhaps it first came out of exhausted and overpopulated India, where the Lord Buddha decided long ago that life was a mess. The religion of despair often achieves a stoical and ascetic nobility, very impressive to those who are impressed by dramatic gestures. Yet it is the very opposite of the true gospel. The Christian gives up his own desires for the love of others; the Eastern ascetic renounces the world because he thinks himself too good for it.

Pride aping love — it is the devil's best trick. Self-mutilation has masqueraded as Christianity; Manichaeism (the notion that the devil created matter) has masqueraded as Christianity; neurotic hatred of life has masqueraded as Christianity. To this day we find men who call themselves Christians maintaining that anything a human being enjoys by nature must be labeled evil.

Why do we so make war upon the gifts of God? We may guess at our own motives: the despair that hates other men's hope, the lovelessness that would deny other men love, the plain vulgar envy and malice that can't bear to see other men happy. For self-denial, there is a philosophical justification — only when duty is unpleasant can we be sure that we're doing it for its own sake and not out of selfishness. Yet to this chilly righteousness the Christian may answer in the words of Augustine: "Have charity and do what you like." And for "others-denial" — for robbing other people of harmless pleasures — there is no justification at all. One fact must be faced honestly by all true Christians: an impulse to spoil others' fun comes straight from the devil.

The negative Sabbath of modern times seems to have originated in the bitter religious strife of the seventeenth century. In Scotland, at that time, one poor wretch was haled into court for *smiling* on the Sabbath; considering the state of Scotland in his day, he should have been congratulated for managing to smile at all. And when the Pilgrims founded their theocratic colony, it seemed quite natural to them to enforce piety by every possible means. People were punished both for not going to church and for going anywhere else. To this day, one sometimes finds the unthinkingly devout extolling the sort of "religion" produced by such methods.

Every church, always, must wrestle with the temptation of *forcing* people to come to God. Force is such an easy and obvious means! As long as one can use force, one need not interest men, need not inspire them, need not humble oneself to be amiable and cajoling — the poor wretches have no escape. They are in the truest sense a "captive audience." The trouble is that a captive audience is a very different thing from a church.

In other words, churches that use force destroy themselves and their goal. During our early history nonattendance at church was punishable by law. When the public conscience revolted at this, some churchmen resorted to *indirect* force; they no longer insisted that men attend — but they saw to it that all other places a man could go were closed. If this seems a justifiable expedient, let us remember that in the early years of industrialism working people had hardly any free time except on Sunday; when nineteenth century Sabbatarians denied men recreation on the Lord's Day, they came close to denying it altogether.

No doubt their intentions were good. Yet what has the end been? A materialist generation and a secularized Sabbath. Whenever churchmen ruled out one of mankind's earthly joys as unholy, they narrowed the scope of holiness. It was inevitable that ultimately everything worth doing should be regarded as purely secular; and that God himself, by fugitives from negative religion, should be conceived, not as the Source of joy, but as a foe of all joy.

How, then, may the churches recapture Sunday?

They will never recapture it, if they think of churchgoing itself as the goal. God is the goal. If we believe in him at all, we must believe that every man wants God in his heart far more than he can ever want anything else; that is, every man wants peace and love, answers to his questions, and the keys of heaven. When a church gives these, its doors overflow.

When it does not — well, though it speak with the tongues of popular psychologists and radio commentators, though it make donations to hospitals and conduct political forums, it avails nothing.

How do you make a day holy? By stopping work — that is, by stopping all the pursuits we engage in for necessity not for pleasure, all our struggles with the world conceived as an enemy that is trying to starve us to death. By looking at that world and seeing that it is good. By entering into all its good and friendly and loving activities, and rejoicing in them. And, above all, by looking beyond the world to the Love that sustains it.

It is very hard, all the same, to tell the churches what to do with the Sabbath; much easier to tell them what *not* to do. It is easy to say: "Stop kicking against the pricks. Stop making a fuss over this or that bit of Sunday levity. Stop trying to force or terrify or bribe men into attendance. A forced churchgoer has no religion, a terrified churchgoer has no Christianity, a bribed churchgoer has no morals. We don't want men who come to church because the golf course is closed, but men who prefer God to golf."

All this is very true, but not very constructive. Similarly, there is not much value in drawing up a point-to-point program for spending the Sabbath devoutly. A formal service in the morning, informal prayer meetings or question-answering sessions or church outings later, would no doubt make a good day. But we have all these things already, often very well organized, and yet they don't seem to draw the crowd. It might help if we thought less of the dignity of divine worship, and more of the sheer fun of it; if we took over all God's pleasures of body and mind and showed how, rightly used, they are faint foreshadowings of the supreme pleasure. Perhaps what we need, in this connection, is to revive the ancient concepts of sacred dances and sacred games. A well-organized church festival of sport and music and theatricals would certainly be more attractive to many people than the disorganized and murderous traffic of our Sunday highways.

But in the end the church must stand or fall by the church-men.

Most of the ordinary people who lose their faith are not overthrown by philosophical argument; they lose faith because they are disillusioned by the churchmen they meet. One sanctimonious hypocrite makes a hundred unbelievers. One little knot of gossips tearing a neighbor's reputation apart on the church steps smashes the Sabbath to splinters. If we are to put it together again, we must be Christians indeed — must show the rest of the world that a Christian gets something worth having out of his worship. It is not much use asking others to turn to God unless we set them the example. Let the church members behave like Christians seven days a week, and it is likely that the Sabbath will take care of itself. For how do you make a day holy? By seeing that it is holy already; and behaving accordingly.

V

THE SERPENT'S TOOTH

Honor thy father and thy mother: that thy days may be long upon the land which the Lord thy God giveth thee.
— Ex. 20:12.

ONCE UPON A TIME there was a little old man. His eyes blinked and his hands trembled; when he ate he clattered the silverware distressingly, missed his mouth with the spoon as often as not, and dribbled a bit of his food on the tablecloth. Now he lived with his married son, having nowhere else to live, and his son's wife was a modern young woman who knew that in-laws should not be tolerated in a woman's home.

"I can't have this," she said. "It interferes with a woman's right to happiness."

So she and her husband took the little old man gently but firmly by the arm and led him to the corner of the kitchen. There they set him on a stool and gave him his food, what there was of it, in an earthenware bowl. From then on he always ate in the corner, blinking at the table with wistful eyes.

One day his hands trembled rather more than usual, and the earthenware bowl fell and broke.

"If you are a pig," said the daughter-in-law, "you must eat out of a trough." So they made him a little wooden trough, and he got his meals in that.

These people had a four-year-old son of whom they were very fond. One suppertime the young man noticed his boy playing intently with some bits of wood and asked what he was doing.

"I'm making a trough," he said, smiling up for approval, "to feed you and Mamma out of when I get big."

The man and his wife looked at each other for a while and

didn't say anything. Then they cried a little. Then they went to the corner and took the little old man by the arm and led him back to the table. They sat him in a comfortable chair and gave him his food on a plate, and from then on nobody ever scolded when he clattered or spilled or broke things.

One of Grimm's fairy tales, this anecdote has the crudity of the old simple days; the modern serpent's tooth method would be to lead Grandpa gently but firmly to the local asylum, there to tuck him out of sight as a case of senile dementia. But perhaps crudity is what we need to illustrate the naked and crude point of the Fifth Commandment: honor your parents lest your children dishonor you. Or, in other words, a society that destroys the family destroys itself.

Does this seem too selfish an interpretation of the law? Nowadays we sometimes like to get rid of the Commandments by broadening them into lofty moral sentiments too vague to apply in daily life. Thus "Honor your father and mother" is often broadened into something like, "We have a collective responsibility for the aged," which, though perfectly true, can in practice be used to evade our individual responsibility for our own old folks — to justify treating our parents with the same cold benevolence we feel toward indigent strangers in a home for the aged. We plume ourselves on having eliminated selfishness and narrowness from the Decalogue by lifting it above the sphere of personal human contacts; but we have only eliminated reality, for all principles of conduct must come down in the end to the actual relations of flesh-and-blood people. And we have forgotten that the Commandments are not a set of divine ethical abstractions, but a set of quite practical rules for getting along in a very rough world. One reason for being nice to Father is clearly stated in terms of naked self-interest: "That thy days may be long."

Fathers had remarkable powers when the Fifth Commandment was first written. They were not only heads of families but heads of governments — military leaders, judges, priests;

the Bedouin sheik is perhaps the nearest contemporary equivalent. They could kill with the sword, kill with the law, or kill with a curse, and their rights over their children were mystical and absolute. Thus, though much is said about Abraham's suffering over sacrificing Isaac and Jephthah's over sacrificing his daughter, the Old Testament never questions their *right* to do it. And thus, when criminals are condemned, the Pentateuch usually takes it for granted that their children and grandchildren shall perish with them, as being in some mystical way parts of their bodies.

All this may seem sheer barbarity to us, unless we make some effort to understand how tribesmen think. They don't think in modern terms about the importance of the individual; indeed, to some modern students it seems as if the tribesman had no consciousness of his individual self at all, as if he were aware of himself *only* in his relation to the clan, like a bee in a beehive. This is surely an exaggeration, for all men since the beginning have had self-consciousness — in fact, self-consciousness is a prerequisite of original sin. Nevertheless it is true that the tribesman thinks of his identity as clan member as the important thing; what he is in *himself* is secondary. And his view is perfectly sensible, for he can survive only as a clan member. Once outcast from the tribe, thrown back on his own poor personality, he finds every man's hand against him and he must perish, unless the Almighty give him a mark like Cain's for protection. So too the clan itself, if disunited and fatherless, goes down to destruction. In such a world men must honor their fathers or their days will be " poor, nasty, brutish, and short "!

To clan society, therefore, a man is not so much himself as the son of his father. He is Abdul ibn Yusuf ibn Mahmud, Joseph ben Jacob ben Isaac, Ivan Ivanovitch, O'Brien or MacGregor or Gaius of the Caesar family of the clan Julia descended from Venus; he is one of the children of Abraham or the sons of Atreus; he is true Anglo-Saxon or " *echt Deutsch* " or even (for clan thinking dies hard) 100 per cent American. When, at the climax of his history, he is Jesus who calls himself the Son of Man, he is making a statement which is at once clear to the clansmen, though for the modern individualist it perhaps needs the translation that we are all members one or another.

The absolutism of the clan father was often cruel, but it had a limiting factor: to the clan, children were an inestimable asset. Nowadays we take it for granted that our young are a financial burden, but in Old Testament days they were a form of wealth and power. Job's large family is listed with his flocks and herds among the signs of his prosperity. In that world a man was not fully a man till he begot a son, a sterile woman was considered accursed, and children were the very meaning of life. How little Job would have understood the view of some "enlightened moderns" that children are an *interference* with one's own life!

Thus even a selfish father could be trusted to look after his young fairly well — according to his lights — for his own sake, as a modern woman tends her washing machine or a modern man his car. And if people were to survive at all, either as individuals or as families, they must be taught to honor their parents with unquestioning loyalty and obedience.

Contrast this patriarchal world with the civilization of imperial Rome! By the time of Saint Paul, the Mediterranean basin was overpopulated; desperate methods of preventing childbearing had come into fashion; family life was rapidly breaking down. The satires of Juvenal show us a society whose vices are horribly familiar. It was no longer possible to take it for granted that parents meant well. When Paul, in the Epistle to the Ephesians, restated the Fifth Commandment, he thought it advisable to add, "And, ye fathers, provoke not your children to wrath"!

If we are to make sense of the Commandment today, we must begin with Paul's addition. For there is no denying that our society often sins against the children. Everybody today — Fascists and Communists and all of us in-betweens — will agree that family life is indispensable to human health and happiness. Yet we find ourselves accepting conditions that make war on the family. The lands behind the Iron Curtain deliberately weaken family ties in their schools, lest loyalty to parents should conflict with devotion to the sacred State. Our own country tries to keep the home fires burning with verbal sentiment about Mom, but meanwhile forces Mom to leave the hearth fire untended while she tends the factory machine. A century ago, American houses were twelve-room affairs designed to hold grandparents, and maiden aunts, and uncles, as well as parents and children; today they are usually cramped little flats and cottages, and we feel lucky to get those. We can hardly do much about honoring Father and Mother if there's no room for them in the inn.

No doubt the breakdown of family ties which so alarms modern America is largely the result of industrialism. For in an industrial world the family ceases to be economically efficient; it is no longer a way of making money. In place of the home workshop we have factory and supermarket and office. Once there were a hundred kinds of shared creation that bound parents and children together: spinning, weaving, baking breads, clothing the household and making its furniture, brewing beer, and curing meat — all these in addition to the particular trade in which the family specialized. The old taught and governed the young; the young honored the old for their knowledge and at the same time learned to respect themselves as responsible and useful members of a household. But all this creative work has now been taken away and parceled out among the men who serve the Machine. Housework today has been reduced to a dull and crude sort of labor, tiring but unrewarding, which bores the average housewife so much that she has to listen to the radio to take her mind off it. What sort of rich human experience can a child get on such terms?

Only on our farms are children still really valuable workers, and perhaps that is why the old-fashioned, closely knit family survives on our farms more than elsewhere. As for the city crowd — well, the family may still be necessary to happiness, but it's only a nuisance to the purse, and people easily come to believe, in a satirist's phrase: " What good is happiness? You can't buy money with it! "

People easily come to believe things that destroy them; as, for instance, " Whatever is profitable must be right." There is no real need for defeatism about the family. We might very well, if we would, manage to reconcile the happy family with the industrial system; we could disperse our industries, spread out our homes in garden towns, say no to everything that denies a child freedom of motion and the companionship of his parents. Clear heads among us do this for themselves — there are plenty of " child-centered homes " even today. What stops the rest of us? An airy nothing, a climate of opinion, a complacent belief that things are all right as they are, that civilization and progress consist in having the State do as much as possible and the home as little as possible — in short, that the less family life we have, the better.

Every age has its professional apologists, and ours are working hard to convince us that our worst sins are virtues. A mother forced to take a job needs a crèche for her baby, admitted — but that does not justify the false comforters who tell us a crèche is better than a mother. An overcrowded school must pick up its pupils in large handfuls all of an age, and pass them along without paying attention to their individual abilities — yet this hardly warrants the current theory that children *ought* to be herded in age groups, as if we gave birth to them in litters! The cooped-up small families of cities are likely to develop unhealthy tensions, as we all know — need we, therefore, swallow the fashionable psychological doctrine that it's natural for all sons to hate their fathers? Were it really true that sons and fathers are natural enemies, how could mankind ever have dreamed of such a thing as the Fatherhood of God?

Through such apologies, and our own mental laziness, we are in danger of accepting without question some very queer distortions of human life. Already our generations are being walled off from each other: teen-agers flock together deaf to all language but their own, young couples automatically drop their unmarried friends, whole magazines address themselves to age groups such as the seventeens or the young matrons or the "older executive type." Vast numbers of people think it "natural" to hate your in-laws, "immature" to ask your parents for advice after your marriage, "abnormal" to value the companionship of anyone much older or younger than yourself. And a thousand stories and articles testify to one of the greatest problems of American life: father and son, mother and daughter, cannot talk to one another with understanding.

Of course the modern way, the collectivism into which we are all being forced willy-nilly, does have certain advantages. When community and State take over responsibility, children and the aged are no longer wholly dependent on the sometimes doubtful devotion of their blood kin. When education and social services are a State rather than a private concern, we escape the narrowness and hatred of clan life, in which "stranger" means "enemy" — we get that much nearer to realizing the brotherhood of man. A couple of centuries back there was a family of distinguished surgeons that invented the obstetrical forceps and jealously guarded it as a trade secret; *that* sort of family loyalty we are much better off without.

Still we are paying too high a price for our gains, paying in terms of juvenile delinquency and adult unhappiness, for those who have never known warmth and love when they were small are seldom capable of much love when they grow big. We pay in restlessness, in desperate pleasure-seeking, in the lack of moral standards — our teeth are set on edge by the sour grapes of our fathers' eating. No gain in social efficiency can save a community that offends against the little ones. And let us be honest about it: our modern cities have created a society in which children are in the way.

They are physically in the way, and therefore we find them in the way emotionally too. There are many who do not want them at all, like the girl who recently told this writer that a civilized woman can "realize her creative impulses through self-expression" without needing anything so dirty as a baby! Even those who do want them are sometimes rather shame-faced about it; pregnancy, once something in which a woman gloried, is now treated as a disfigurement to be concealed as long as possible; and giving suck, the greatest joy and greatest need of both mother and child, is quite out of fashion among us. "I'm not a cow!" some American women will remark scornfully, as if it were preferable to be a fish.

Worse yet, perhaps, is the taming process we are forced to put our children through in order to keep them alive at all in city streets and city flats. In their infancy we must curb their play, and force adult cautions and restraints on them too soon; in their adolescence, on the other hand, we must bend all our efforts to keep them children at an age when our ancestors would have recognized them as grown men and women ready to found families. Our objection to child labor is admirable when it prevents the exploitation of babies in sweatshops, but not when it keeps vigorous young men and women frittering away their energies on meaningless school courses and still more meaningless amusements. Many an eighteen-year-old has declared bitterly that the only time society recognizes him as a man is when it needs him to go out and fight.

For all this we may offer the excuse of economic compulsion. We have created machines; machines have replaced human labor; a new pair of hands, therefore, is not an asset but a liability.

Our ancestors were quite as sinful as we are; if their family life worked better, on the whole, it was less by virtue than by necessity. Taken as practical counsel for survival, the Fifth Commandment is now almost a dead letter. Yet if our world were truly Christian, the change might be a reason for rejoicing. We no longer *need* our families — we are therefore free to love them with complete unselfishness. Now at last we might do for love what our ancestors did for self-interest; now at last it is possible to honor our parents genuinely, because they no longer have the power to kill us if we don't. The old sort of honor was sometimes an ugly sham — the son who respects Father only out of fear of punishment is not much of a son, just as the Christian who worships God only out of fear of hell is precious little of a Christian. But the new sort of honor can be a beautiful and holy thing. There are many sweet and sane families bound together by love; there are plenty of experts who remind us that only love can make the modern family work at all. And one must admit that there are plenty of parents very willing to be honored.

The catch is that not so many of them are willing to be honorable. We find our children physically and emotionally in the way, and in consequence often offend against them by denying them real parents. Once for all: if we wish our children to honor us, we must ourselves set the example of honor. Let us drop the pretense that a sane man can or should honor the dishonorable and love the unlovely. He must indeed love the sinner, but let him not forget to hate the sin; let him not teach children to think that a petty tyrant is a good father, a drunken slut a devoted mother. If we order the child to blind himself to his parents' faults, we are forcing him to acquire those faults himself. Everyone knows at least one parent who, at a breath of criticism or independence, appeals dramatically to the Fifth Commandment and mutters about the serpent's tooth and the thankless child; who demands constant gratitude for having done no more than his (or, more usually, her) biological and legal duty; who feels entitled to monopolize the lives of grown children "in return for all I went through to bring you up." In that much misunderstood play *King Lear*, Shakespeare deals with the parent who tries to bribe or bully his way to honor — pillories him for all time as the pitiful egoist he is. Everyone knows him; and everyone knows, too, that in actual fact he has usually been a very bad parent indeed. Serpents beget serpents after their kind, and the sharpest serpent's tooth of all belongs to the parent without love.

"Provoke not your children to wrath." Easily said; but how are we to avoid it? Strife between old and young seems inevitable. Today the world changes fast and inconceivably fast; in pastoral and agricultural times, what a man knew was of use to his son, but in the industrial age Father's knowledge is out of date before the son is half grown up. We should be more than human if the result were not bitterness and conflict. Then too there are just too many people on this teeming and screaming earth for us to welcome a new man with whole-souled enthusiasm. Our God-given biologic nature, which rejoices in parenthood, and our fallen self-seeking nature, which hates it as the creator of responsibilities, are at war with each other; and if we cannot make peace with ourselves, how shall we make peace with our children?

The ideal solution, of course, would be to remake our jerry-built, precarious society into a sound and safe one. But, let's admit it, we don't know how; and if we knew, we have not the power; and if we had the power, as long as we are sinners we should lack the love. There is only one thing a man can really remake — himself — and that only with the aid of God's grace. Laws and organizations and schools are good things, crèches and social services and youth groups may be admirable things. Yet — a reminder obvious, trite, but necessary — none of them can replace the love and guidance of father and mother. Our problem, then, pending reconstruction of the world, is to reconstruct our own lives so that we give our children as much warmth and attention and time and teaching as the present world will allow.

At least we might give them our leisure. Let us drop the disastrous cant that persuades women, often against their own hearts, that they have a " duty " to neglect their children for civic affairs, or broadening cultural activities, or even, heaven help us, for "realizing their creative potentialities through self-expression in a rewarding career." Let us drop too the curious theory that the care and teaching of children are entirely women's work, and that their father should have as little to do with them as possible. Most of all, let us remind the innumerable Americans who don't seem to know it that begetting and rearing a family are far more real and rewarding than making and spending money.

And we might, as some towns do, train our high school

students in caring for children as we train them in stenography and driving cars. And we might make the home a center of Christian worship and education. But all this will not serve unless the heart is changed. New England homes have traditionally been centers of Christian worship; nevertheless the New England poet Robert Frost could write bitterly, "Home is the place where, when you have to go there, they have to take you in."

That is the best it can ever be, without love. Let us, then, practice and pray for love, and the honor will take care of itself.

VI

WHO TAKE THE SWORD

Thou shalt not kill. — Ex. 20:13.

SEVERAL YEARS AGO a few young men in a plane dropped a bomb that blasted about fifty thousand Japanese to death. Afterward they came home, somewhat embarrassed to find themselves temporarily famous. They were wined and dined, they were asked questions about their emotions and pursued with flash bulb and camera. Eventually one of those ladies whom the press calls "leading Washington hostesses" gave them a reception, whose most notable feature was an elaborately iced cake in the shape of an atomic explosion.

It was news, that cake; or at least it was a novelty, which for many of our newspapers comes to the same thing. The picture went all over the nation — the Air Force man looking uncomfortable with a cake knife, the hostess smirking, the sugar and flour monstrosity bursting into a mushroom cloud. Thereupon the conscience of America, already uneasily sparking and fizzing, reached critical mass and produced a very pretty little explosion of its own.

No matter what we were — pacifist or militarist, civilian or soldier, Red or Red-baiter — we all hated that cake. It was one of the few things the public opinion of this diverse and diffuse country has even been able to agree on completely. For whatever our personal beliefs may be, we are still by inheritance part of Christendom. And to Christendom, to the world that accepts or once did accept the Sermon on the Mount as its law, that cake was an obscenity. Christians differ as to whether or not they may in some circumstances kill; they do not differ about whether they may gloat over a fallen enemy. To this day America has not been able to reach agree-

71

ment on whether the bombing of Hiroshima was necessary. But one thing we'll all agree to: necessary or not, it wasn't funny.

That public explosion of horror was the law speaking through us — the Commandment that told us long ago that we must not murder. Heartening that it spoke so loudly, good to know that a secularist age has kept so much of Christian decency! Yet perhaps there was a touch of the Pharisee in our indignation. Perhaps we were hoping to excuse the beam of mass murder in the national eye by yammering over the mote of bad taste in the eye of one silly woman. Perhaps, indeed, we were trying to buy easy consciences dirt cheap. For though we condemned the cake, we did not abandon the bomb.

And we have not succeeded in easing our consciences. Every time we read of a new improvement in atomic destruction, we feel worse, no matter whether the improvement is ours or our rival's. At this moment we hold the bomb poised ready to throw, paralyzed in mid-action by — what? Fear; fear of retaliation, fear of smashing the world, fear of the condemnation of mankind, and, let us hope, fear of God.

Forget the bomb. It is used here merely as a symbol; this most spectacular of human murder methods, and the spectacular hysteria it provokes in so many, may serve to illustrate our terrifying inner confusion over the Sixth Commandment. We have a million other methods of killing, and we are confused about them all. May we kill men at all, and if we may, when and why? When is killing murder? And can a man commit murder, morally speaking, by an act of omission — by selling inflammable sweaters, for instance, or deathtrap cars, or useless medicines, or even by passing by on the other side of the road while thieves are butchering someone? And what of those who never do physical harm, but who spend their lives twisting and bullying wives or children or employees out of all human shape — what of the killers of the soul?

We have laws to answer some of these questions; but laws seem achingly inadequate in a world of fire and blood and the breaking of nations. We have civilized scruples too; the articulate among us, jurists and teachers and writers, often treat violence as a bad word, a thing shocking and unnatural, to be hidden from innocent children and discussed only in sick whispers — very much, in fact, as the Victorians treated sex. No previous age has ever equaled our horror of killing, but then, no previous age ever killed so much.

Originally, of course, the Sixth Commandment meant only to forbid murder — the private and unjustified erasure of your enemies. Our standard versions of the Bible mistranslate it, for scholars will tell us that both Hebrew and Greek, both Old Testament and New, actually use the word for "murder" in this context and not the word for "kill." Too obvious, too limited a prohibition, perhaps, for our own time, with its increased awareness of the sanctity of human life — and its morbid fear of death. But imagine what the dawn ages must have been like. Imagine man as a dangerous animal, to whom killing came as naturally as breathing; a creature that clawed and bit and clubbed automatically to get what he wanted, or to remove an annoyance, or even because he liked the way it made him feel.

By the time the Hebrews got as far as writing down their law, they were fairly civilized, and they had centuries of other men's civilizations and legal codes behind them. The traditional history recorded in the Old Testament, nevertheless, indicates that killing was still one of the ordinary pleasures of life. How the ancient Jews did slaughter! They killed in hot blood and in cold; they killed for loot, for God, and for fun. To spare prisoners of war and their women and children was considered almost blasphemy. "Go and utterly destroy the sinners!" says the Lord to Saul, and when the warrior king tries to spare Agag, the priest and prophet Samuel defends religion by chopping the helpless captive to bits. "Sun, stand thou still upon Gibeon," commands Joshua, lest the killing might have to stop. Nor was war the only form of the pastime. The tribes killed by trickery and riotous massacre, as in The Book of Esther; by wholesale legal extermination, as

when Joshua finished off Achan and his sons and daughters;
by political assassination, as when Ehud stabbed King Eglon
in his fat belly; by violation of hospitality, as when Jael
knocked her tenpenny nail through the sleeping Sisera's
brain; by treachery in love, as when Judith first seduced
Holofernes and then sliced off his head. All these horror
stories, naturally, were never meant to be taken as moral les-
sons, though misguided Christians have occasionally used
them as an evil precedent. They were set down as tribal
legends of the bad old days before the law, when the Jews
were not people of the Book but marauding nomads rather
like the Sioux who finished off Custer at the Little Big Horn.
And their value to us is largely as a grim picture of what all
people are like before God speaks in the thunder on Sinai —
or after they have forgotten what he said.

The definition of murder took shape slowly. For primitive
tribes, killing was murder only within your own clan. The
stranger was fair game — you were normally at war with all
strangers; it was peace that had to be declared, and seldom
was! Cain's offense was not so much killing as killing his
brother. And we still have some sense of the ancient holiness
of blood kinship, for we feel an extra horror of murder within
the family, though it must be admitted that the relatives who
get themselves murdered have usually done rather more to
deserve their end than the strangers who are murdered for
profit. Yet in some ways our view is the very antithesis of the
tribesman's. We may sometimes extenuate the killing of an
unspeakable parent; we can never sympathize with the
slaughter of one's own helpless child. To our kinsmen three
thousand years back, on the other hand, even accidental parricide was the supreme abomination, whereas killing one's
own child was not a crime at all.

Thus we cannot understand the full effect of the Sixth Commandment without going behind it to the sort of law it super-
seded: such law as Hammurabi's of Babylon.

"If a man strike a gentleman's daughter that she dies, his

own daughter is to be put to death; if a poor man's, the slayer pays one half mina."

For Hammurabi and his times, the individual and individual guilt were nothing, the loss in value to the clan or family the sole consideration. The *lex talionis* — "An eye for an eye, and a tooth for a tooth" — is barbarous enough; yet in its day it was an advance over the indiscriminate slaughter of the offender and all his household in vengeance for a single injury, intentional or not. The *lex talionis* does not so much prescribe punishment as limit revenge. And it is the usual law of the Old Testament; still, with the Sixth Commandment, it is at least partly replaced by something better. For the first time, murder is conceived, not as a natural privilege, to be paid for in blood money if necessary, but as a moral transgression. And for the first time it dawns upon man that one ought to consider not only the harm done but also the harm intended; that killing a man by accident when the head flies off your ax is not the same thing as killing him in order to steal his wife. What though the Pentateuch definition of murder is narrow? The important thing is to get murder defined at all; to convince men that they mustn't stab one another for no better reason than whim or appetite. Nowadays we are given to thinking that all killing is bad, and it may seem shockingly inadequate for the Sixth Commandment to tell us that not all killing is good. But for the noble savage it was quite a new and strange idea.

Savage they were, those ancient Hebrews, but for the most part healthy and brave and sane; men who liked to fight, who accepted struggle as the very meaning of life, who thought of safety as something fit only for women and eunuchs. "Man is born unto trouble, as the sparks fly upward," they said, and shrugged, and enjoyed themselves. Their appetite for slaughter needed restraining exactly like a child's appetite for lollipops.

By the time of the Captivity they were greatly changed. They were a beaten people, their Temple ruined, their clans

disorganized, their families scattered; they were so dispirited
that they seem almost modern. When Nehemiah wanted them
to rebuild Jerusalem's defenses, he reassured them about their
enemies:

"Be not ye afraid of them: remember the Lord, which is
great and terrible, and fight for your brethren, your sons, and
your daughters, your wives, and your houses. . . .

"In what place therefore ye hear the sound of the trumpet,
resort ye thither unto us: our God shall fight for us."

But they were beaten again and again after that. Babylonian, Persian, Greek, and Syrian trampled them; the glorious
explosion of the Maccabees was their last real triumph; their
best weapons and their best courage were no more than
pitiful straws against the iron legions and law of Rome. There
was no longer any sane hope of independence, but perhaps
defeated men can never be quite sane, and these had defeat
festering in their minds like unreconstructed Southerners or
Germans after the Versailles Treaty. They dreamed of revenge, of a messiah, a prince of war, who would smash the
enemies they could not smash for themselves. Blind with
hatred, they rejected the good of the Pax Romana along with
the evil; and even their law, once a meaningful relation
with God, had become corrupted into pointless rituals and ta-
boos, cherished mainly as a reassurance that they were indeed
different from other people, a true superrace.

It was the moment for a miracle, a new revelation. The
Prince of Peace was born.

What did he tell them, those bitter brooding men? Not,
certainly, what they most wanted to hear — that God would
give them their revenge and tread down their enemies like
grapes in a winepress. Fear of reprisals kept them from doing much actual killing, but they had one comfort: they could
nurse bloody thoughts of what they'd *like* to do to the Romans.
They could dream of chopping taxgatherers into little bits, or
ravaging the white new Greek cities that shone so impudently
on the shores of Galilee. Then along came a man from Nazareth who told them that they must forgive their enemies!

Not enough, he said, to stop short of murder. A man must not use the machinery of law for his revenges, must not even take vengeance with a slanderous tongue. Not enough to refrain from open injuries; a man must not cherish a secret anger. Not enough, perhaps, even to forgive, if forgiveness be no more than a cold and passive toleration of the wrong. A man who wants to enter the Kingdom must love his enemies and do them good.

A parenthesis may be needed here. Many moderns interpret the sayings of our Lord as counsels of pacifism, forbidding us ever to kill at all. Take such remarks as "Turn the other cheek!" out of context, and they can easily be made over into the Eastern doctrine of nonresistance so appealing to tired men. Yet remember that Jesus said, "Thou shalt not murder," and not, "Thou shalt not kill." Elsewhere too he spoke as if the use of force could be lawful; he came not to bring peace but a sword, he praised the Roman centurion whose sword brought order, and he scourged the money-changers out of the Temple. What he forbade, then, was not violence, but self-seeking violence; not anger, but being angry without cause. He laid upon us the duty of protecting the weak, and it is obviously impossible to do that without sometimes having to fight the strong. Perhaps Jesus is admired as pacifist chiefly by those who have ceased to believe in him as God.

For we others — we who accept the resurrection and its victory over death — know that death of the body is not the supreme evil; damnation of the soul is that. We do not imagine that Christ's mission on earth was to prevent our natural bodies from getting knocked to bits — since in any case that which we sow is not quickened unless it die. It follows that killing a man is not the worst thing you can do to him or yourself; indeed, killing a man may often not be an evil at all.

Beware, though, of the figurative approach that declares that various cruelties and spites and subtle persecutions are "really" murder much more than shooting a man through the head in a fit of temper. These things may well be worse than murder, but they are not murder, and to call them so metaphorically can result only in making the word useless for any practical purpose.

And heaven knows the subject is confused enough already. Christendom, following its Master, has long tried to distinguish between killings intentional and accidental, justified and unjustified; in consequence we have been forced to multiply laws, to elaborate definitions, to make wild and presumptuous guesses about what goes on in a human mind when it decides to kill. We have never quite known what to do about murderers by willful negligence or omission — hit-run drivers, say, or company directors who save money on safeguards and send miners to agonizing death. Such big fish may often get away while we deal with the sprats, and people remark cynically that justice is blind. We could use a good method of trapping the indirect private killer, certainly; for that matter, we are not particularly good at catching the direct one — this country has a frighteningly high murder rate, and it is often asserted that about sixty per cent of our killings go unsolved. American lawlessness, deservedly or not, is a by-word among the nations, and it must trouble our consciences deeply whenever we reflect on the Commandment, "Thou shalt not kill."

Nor are our unwarranted killings confined to actual law-breaking. Anyone who studies our poisonous drugs, our denatured food, our deathtrap automobiles and houses, our lung-rotting cities, must conclude that we accept a good deal of murder as inevitable simply because it is done to make or save money.

Meanwhile we have seen the heads of European states slaughter whole populations, and it is not surprising if we are confused about where murder stops and legitimate war begins. The Chaplin film *Monsieur Verdoux,* in which a Bluebeard killer defended himself on the ground that nations make war, is a good example of the prevailing muddle; there are many who feel that the only way to abolish murder public or private is to abolish violence altogether — rather like reasoning that the only way to abolish indigestion is to do away with food.

The use of force, after all, is a natural and necessary function of man in this dangerous world.

For the present outburst of destruction, no doubt, secularism may be partly to blame. A man cannot obey a law he has never learned, and the failure of our education to give adequate moral and spiritual training is too well known to need discussion here, Lacking belief in the promises and commandments of God, one must fall back on a "man-centered" philosophy — something called humanism or materialism, which accepts this life and its immediate desires as the basis of all conduct. And you can't get a moral law out of materialism. There is no logical reason why a materialist shouldn't poison his nagging wife, if he can get away with it.

The essential amorality of all atheist doctrines is often hidden from us by an irrelevant personal argument. We see that many articulate secularists are well-meaning and law-abiding men; we see them go into righteous indignation over injustice and often devote their lives to good works. So we conclude that "he can't be wrong whose life is in the right" — that their philosophies are just as good guides to action as Christianity. What we don't see is that they are not acting on their philosophies. They are acting, out of habit or sentiment, on an inherited Christian ethic which they still take for granted though they have rejected the creed from which it sprang. Their children will inherit somewhat less of it.

The feeble unreality of materialism has never been better shown than in its failure to cope with killing. Christian doctrine is tough and realistic; it admits the fallen nature of man and his powerful animal impulses, and sets to work to teach him control and direction. But the humanist, the man worshiper, can only play ostrich. To him, man is intrinsically good; or, as he would say, constructive. Therefore, if people turn out to have destructive impulses, these must be the result of faulty education, or of slum conditions, or of diseased economic systems, or even of comic books. Well-intentioned materialists will actually argue that *all* murderers are, *ipso facto,* insane. And they will urge us to prevent our children from ever learning about violence by censoring their reading, emasculating their fairy tales. In the latest version, the wolf no longer eats Ridinghood's grandmother, and records croon to us of the "Three Kind Mice" who

> "All ran after the farmer's wife,
> Who cut them some cheese with a carving knife."

Did you ever hear such a tale in your life?

Make no mistake about it; violence is here to stay. All we can accomplish with a blanket condemnation is to widen the gulf between the wild and the tame humans — between the lawless materialists who kill when they should not and the nice little humanists who can't kill when they should. Squeamishness about physical force is not virtue; our Lord implied as much when he classed spiritual nastinesses — spite and contention and vindictiveness — along with murder. We do not make a better world by training the fight out of our little boys; we only make a more cowardly one — a world of murderees inviting the murderer. And the result of arguing that *all* violence is horrid, as always with all-or-nothing doctrines, is to produce a hysterical alternation of all *and* nothing; thus the Hindu either renounces mating entirely or breeds like the rabbits of Australia, either spares the life of his body lice or throws the neighboring Mohammedan's children down a well. And thus our Western world, faced today with an overpopulation it cannot or will not control, alternates between frenzied massacre and a blind insistence on prolonging all human lives as much as possible, no matter how they hurt.

Here we come upon the chief cause of modern killing and modern guilt. It would be dishonest and shallow to lay the whole blame on materialism, though it is true that materialism can inspire men with an indecent love of their own lives and an indecent indifference to the lives of others. It is true that men cannot obey a law they have not learned; as Saint Paul pointed out, however, neither can they succeed in obeying a law they *have* learned. After all, the devout Christian ages murdered in private and massacred wholesale in war, just as we do. Whatever their creed, men are tempted to kill when several of them want the same thing. If the thing is not important in itself — say, a given town, a given job, a given woman — they may be brought to see reason and accept a peaceful compromise. But what if the thing they want is food?

Today there are too many people and not enough food. Never mind why; never mind what science and common sense may conceivably be able to do about it someday. At present the problem exists. The haves, like ourselves, are forced to defend their dinner tables against the have-nots. And "Thou shalt not kill" raises a dreadful political question. Unwarlike America, trying more or less to live by the Decalogue, finds itself compelled to kill those who live by no law except force.

We do on occasion kill them — with atom bomb or Tommy gun, what difference? — but we do not feel easy about it, and it is well that we do not. It is well that we should look for a peaceful way out of the mess, trying patience and reasonableness and sharing the food we have and teaching the backward nations to produce their own. Nevertheless we cannot help recognizing, in the "Peace at Any Price!" slogan, an effort of our enemies to turn us into the perfect murderee. Surrender, we know, would solve nothing, would only abandon the world to the horrors and massacres of a peace as bad as any war. We know that, in the end, we may have to fight.

And our consciences are troubled about it, because our consciences are not clear. We are aware that things are amiss with us, that we often do things for mammon's sake and pretend we're doing them for God, that as a nation we are perhaps too rich to get into the Kingdom of Heaven easily. The better Christians we are, the more we have learned to recognize the wickedness of our own hearts, and the less we can take it for granted that our killing in war would be justifiable killing and not a cleverly disguised murder. We are shaken, and rightly, when enemies discredit our fine talk about the brotherhood of man by pointing to our treatment of the Negro. We distrust the nobility of our own desire to protect Korea against an invader, when we catch ourselves grudging the money for a traffic light to protect the local school children. Only a virtuous nation can wage war with clean hands, and we know ourselves to be something less than perfectly virtuous.

Few of us would actually murder our neighbor. But can we acquit ourselves of those other offenses which our Lord compared to murder? Are we free in act and intention of spite and slander, vindictiveness and prejudice and subtle cruelty, profiting by others' pain and passing by on the other side of the road? Are we fit men to purify the world, or would our war be only another massacre, and our conquest another disaster?

Until we have cleaned house at home, nobody will trust us to clean houses abroad — we shall not even trust ourselves. The remedy is in each man's hands; in individual repentance, prayer, and rebirth. What the Sixth Commandment means and does not mean was perhaps never better summed up than in Chesterton's great battle hymn:

> " O God of earth and altar,
>   Bow down and hear our cry;
> Our earthly rulers falter,
>   Our people drift and die;
> The walls of gold entomb us,
>   The swords of scorn divide;
> Take not Thy thunder from us,
>   But take away our pride.

> " From all that terror teaches,
>   From lies of tongue and pen;
> From all the easy speeches
>   That comfort cruel men;
> From sale and profanation
>   Of honor and the sword;
> From sleep and from damnation,
>   Deliver us, good Lord! "

VII

THE ADULTEROUS GENERATION

Thou shalt not commit adultery. — Ex. 20:14.

THERE WAS a man who lived with his wife in a state of the Deep South. Hard-working, respectable people they were, good church members, well liked in the community. Everyone was astonished when one day they were thrown into jail for "criminal converse." These two, it seemed, had both been married before; had gone out West, divorced their respective partners, married each other, and come home with the intention of living happily ever after. But someone had other ideas and started a court action. The case was hotly contested, eventually reaching the Supreme Court, but that body ruled that it had no jurisdiction and the couple sat out their terms in the penitentiary.

There was an actress named Bergman. She changed husbands in mid-career and settled down to raise a family by the new one. Unfortunately the legalities took longer than she expected, and, having impulsively failed to wait for legalities, she found herself with a slightly ill-timed baby, and had courage and decency enough not to suppress the evidence. Result, a storm of condemnation and the end of her American career. All our professional Pharisees united to throw stones at her. For what? The divorce? No; the baby.

There was another actress named Hayworth. *She* changed husbands in mid-career too, acquiring a Mohammedan prince as well as a baby. Presently she shrugged off the prince. But *her* baby had been timed correctly. She was, by the standards currently in vogue, a respectable woman. And she returned to Hollywood in triumph, more of a romantic idol than ever.

Doesn't it seem that, in spite of our occasional bursts of

stone-throwing, we Americans are rather uncertain as to where marriage leaves off and adultery begins?

The Christian definition of adultery seems quite clear and hard. While you have a husband or wife still living, taking a new partner is adultery — and a sin. The legal, secular definition, on the other hand, is more pliable. Taking a new partner is adultery, to the law, only if you have not previously got rid of the old partner in a legally recognized fashion. And to the law adultery is not morally wrong; it is only illegal, a quite different matter. What upsets most of us is that we try to judge by both standards at once; the union that is a sin in the Christian view may be quite respectable in the legal one, and people don't really know whether they are doing right or wrong.

Legality, though, is rapidly becoming the *only* criterion. The union of man and woman is considered "right" if you have a piece of paper to show, "wrong" if you haven't. Yet we cannot even be sure of our legalities. They vary from state to state and from year to year; thousands of Americans are not certain whether they are legally married at all, thousands more may find out they're not if the question ever comes before a judge. In Michigan a devoted couple filed for divorce merely to help a journalist friend to write an article, and were horrified to find themselves divorced without further notice; in New York, where divorce is extremely difficult, there are women who earn their living as professional corespondents. If we cannot agree on a definition of marriage, how are we to define adultery?

Once upon a time the three parties to a marriage were man, wife, and God. Now they are generally considered to be man, wife, and State. Of course the State has a quite legitimate interest in marriage; it must protect the children, it must define the rights and obligations of husbands and wives. But is there any reason why, when the State walks in at the door, God must vanish out of the window? Marriage can easily be *both* a mystical union of two creatures into one flesh and a civil contract. For millions of happily married Christian Americans, it is both. And there are a great many secularist Americans whose honest intention of marriage turns a civil contract into a holy union, instead of leaving it just a business deal.

But what of the rest? of the people who furnish our divorce statistics?

Adultery occurs in many forms. There is the casual love affair, indulged in because a momentary temptation is strong, or because " everybody does it, and I don't think it matters." There is the intense, passionate, long-drawn-out triangle (or even quadrilateral), adorned with conflict and heartbreak. And there is the legalized form, with its rapid and light-hearted changing of partners in the courts. All these, in practice, come to much the same thing: a corruption of the heart, a destruction of the home, an end to love. For the sexual union is a *total* commitment — as mystics used to say, in some ways it prefigures the union with God, demanding a self-surrender only less complete than the surrender to him. And where it is less than total it is hardly worth having — a momentary pleasure, a permanent loneliness.

One new marriage in three will end in divorce, statisticians tell us. How many more break up surreptitiously without aid from the courts, we cannot know. How many simmer in bitterness for years, pretenses at marriage in which both partners pursue their love affairs outside — that we can make a shrewd guess at, if we have any experience of the modern world at all. Some of these couples were cynical from the beginning, no doubt, and sought in marriage only an immediate pleasure or profit. But most of them started with high hopes. *They* were going to have perfect marriages, as advised in the magazines. Must we throw stones at them, these failures in love — these people who attempt again and again something that they hope will be healthy marriage, something that turns out to be only an attack of their chronic adultery?

"An evil and adulterous generation," no doubt. But then, was there ever any other kind?

We are not the first era to make a mess of sexual relations; they've been a mess since Eden. The people who tell you, " It

wasn't like that in *my* young days!" are usually merely finding out rather too late in life what it has always been like.
One may say, in fact, that the mess came before the laws. We
can only conjecture about prehistoric marriage — anthropologists' guesses run all the way from the familiar cartoon of
the cave man conquering his bride with a club to an imagined
matriarchy in which priesthoods of women did about as they
pleased with the terrified male. Either way, possession was
probably nine points of the marriage law. A wife has many
uses in savage life; she chews the tendons for your bowstring,
she sews the skins for your clothes and cover, she pounds
grain for your bread, and cleans and cooks the meat you kill.
So the chances are that once you've got her you keep her as
long as you can stand her, unless, of course, some stronger
male takes her away from you. And there's likely to be a good
deal of tooth and claw about the process.

As times grow more peaceful, marriage by purchase re-
places marriage by capture. From the woman's point of view
this is only partly an improvement. In the old wild days a girl
was at least herself, with her own assets, and if she changed
hands freely at least she went to the better man in a fight.
But in the new tame days a girl became her father's property,
a valuable asset to be exchanged for sheep and oxen and other
useful household beasts; to be served for, twice seven years
if necessary, as Jacob served for Rachel. She was bought and
sold, with or without her consent. Once the man who took
her from her first mate may have been entitled to her in
public opinion, as a conqueror and as the best male avail-
able. But under the purchase system he became a thief, an
offender against property rights, and she, if willing, was an
accomplice in a crime. Somewhere along here the concept of
adultery was born.

" Thou shalt not covet thy neighbor's house . . . thy neighbor's wife, nor his manservant, . . . nor his ox, nor his ass,"
says another Commandment, clearly demonstrating the status
of wives as property. And in Deuteronomy, ch. 22, an explicit
distinction is made between the seduction of a free virgin

and the seduction of a betrothed virgin; the former auto-matically becomes the wife of her seducer once he pays her father a stated price, but the latter is treated as the property of her prospective husband, and consequently the seducer must die. In all this there is no awareness of the identity of women as free agents; only the indignation of a man who dis-covers that he has paid the full market price for what, by his standards, is a damaged article.

Justice and decency, without doubt, were at work here along with property rights, for Deuteronomy exempts from death the raped virgin who "cried, and there was none to save her." And another passage forbids a man who has raped a woman captured in war to sell her afterward as a slave — "because thou hast humbled her." And even the sense of ownership in women had an admixture of something better. For these people the bloodline was of supreme and mystical importance; adultery was wrong because it was the cuckoo's act, leaving your chicks to be reared in another's nest. The point of mating was children; thus if a man died childless, his brother must take the widow and raise substitute heirs, and Onan in Genesis is struck dead for refusing to do so, and Tamar the widow is commended for seducing her father-in-law to produce an heir for her dead husband. This child-centered view of marriage persisted as late as the time of Jesus, as we know from the Sadducees' test question about the seven brothers all of whom married the same woman. It was a view that hardly considered the woman's rights and opinions at all, but only the man's right to produce his own heirs and safeguard his own property. The adultery forbidden in the Seventh Commandment originally meant any infringement of the man's rights — and, possibly, nothing more.

Jesus took this old negative prohibition of adultery and turned it into the positive affirmation of marriage.

In practice, of course, male dominance is always tempered by the undoubted fact that the average man is more or less afraid of his wife. But in theory many ancients seem to have held no misuse of a woman wrong, as long as it did not in-

terfere with another man's rights in her. In much of the
Orient, even into modern times, you could have innumerable
wives and mistreat them in innumerable ways; you could
throw out any woman you got tired of; you could visit a
harlot and feel no guilt, since no man suffered a property loss
thereby. All around little Judea, the Orient rioted and wan-
toned, nor was Judea itself (for all its intense interest in God)
particularly strict in its sexual behavior. The Testaments tell
us a good deal about that. However ready to stone a woman
taken in adultery, the men of the time seem to have taken
their own freedom for granted.

It was this male self-satisfaction which Christ attacked by
defining lust as a certain view of women rather than as a
certain act — "Whosoever looketh on a woman to lust after
her hath committed adultery with her already in his heart."

The naïve and the prudish have sometimes thought he
meant that all erotic desire was bad in itself. To this let his
own words answer — the famous words that call a man and
his wife one flesh. Our Lord's command about marriage was
as sharp and straight as a sword. Your wife is your wife for
good, he said; you can't get rid of her, except for adultery
(and only one Gospel permits even that exception) and a
divorced woman is committing adultery if she remarries. Now
this is a difficult doctrine, as the disciples were the first to
point out. Flesh and blood find it an unbearable doctrine.
And, obviously, it is an incomplete doctrine, for it says nothing
about what constitutes a marriage in the first place, nothing
about marriages ended by act of God, nothing about the
woman's rights of action, and nothing about the status of a
divorced man. All that is left to those who come after. Nevertheless the command is there and it is perfectly clear as far
as it goes. We can only escape it by deciding arbitrarily to
throw out that part of the Gospels as a fake; or else by throwing out the divinity of Christ altogether so that we needn't
obey his commands at all.

With that particular command, the old half-slavish status
of women vanished, and a new concept of womanhood and

wifehood came into the world. Every statement our Lord made about sexuality works to protect women and to awaken men to their own responsibilities. Condemning adultery, he yet forgave the adulteresses who repented and loved God, and denounced the lustful and loveless men who caused them to sin. Perhaps that, in itself, is enough to prove Him more than man. For throughout history even the best of men have usually sought to shift the blame for their sexual weaknesses to the women. "The woman tempted me and I did eat!" cried the father of the tribe, and "The woman tempted me!" has been the cry ever since, whenever someone ate where he should not. True enough, most women try to be as tempting as they can. But what Jesus, and later Paul, pointed out was that, although men are not always free agents in love, they are still on the whole far more free than the women are.

How new — and how appalling — the doctrine of a husband's obligations must have seemed to many early Christians! Jew and Greek divorced at pleasure, and the law of Rome was not unlike the law of Reno. Into this indulgent world tumbled the dreadful statement that a man's wife was neither his property nor his amusement; she was a part of himself, flesh of his flesh, and must be treated accordingly.

Even the disciples were appalled. Even Paul was afraid; the real point of his famous "Better to marry than to burn" passage is that marriage may be no sin but it's certainly a mess of trouble. Elsewhere he exalted wedlock in terms that established it as holy, yet his fear is more remembered than his love. For a moment, however, the Christian world did accept in its full austerity and its full glory our Lord's doctrine of marriage.

Only for a moment. Human weakness and human necessity combined to demand modifications. The historian Gibbon remarks, "The ambiguous word that contains the precept of Christ is flexible to any interpretation that the wisdom of a legislature can demand." Yes, and flexible also to any interpretation that our folly, our sins, and our bad habits can demand.

In the crowded and corrupt Roman world, children had become a burden and pleasure a horror, and extremists in the
Church often reacted by rejecting *all* sexuality as evil. In the
feudal ages, a half-tamed nobility wanted whom it wanted
when it wanted — and the Church, though insisting that
marriage was indissoluble, perforce discovered all manner of
loopholes by which a marriage could be declared void. The
jumble of rules governing holy wedlock — Roman law, Jewish law, canon law, strange blends of the three devised by
Honorius and Theodosius and Justinian — left room for much
sharp practice. Our new legal license will frighten us less if
we read a little history and discover how old it is.

And of course some addition to the doctrine was needed.
There are marriages which *God* puts asunder — cases of
desertion and presumed death, cases of danger to body and
soul, cases where children must be saved at all costs from a
destructive parent. The Church, however reluctantly and sor-
rowfully, always recognized the need for some way out of the
hell of a bad marriage. Paul himself declared, of Christians
married to pagans: "If the unbelieving depart, let him depart. A brother or sister is not under bondage in such cases."

Two thousand years of interpretation — and the upshot
today is that some Churches recognize no divorce at all, some
Churches admit divorce but not remarriage, some Churches
accept divorce and remarriage too. But all unite to condemn
mating that is not sanctified by the intention of marriage,
whether it be fornication, ordinary adultery, or the legalized
adultery which, as we have seen, permits a series of marriages
that are for pleasure and not for life. To quote C. S. Lewis:
"If people do not believe in permanent marriage, it is perhaps better that they should live together unmarried than
than they should make vows they do not mean to keep. It is
true that by living together without marriage they will be
guilty (in Christian eyes) of fornication. But one fault is not
mended by adding another: unchastity is not improved by
adding perjury" (*Mere Christianity,* The Macmillan Company, 1952).

And marriage reduced to no more than a civil contract may easily degenerate into just that — unchastity made respectable by perjury. Thousands of young people today marry with outward hope and love, but with a secret mental reservation — "*if* it works." They may hereafter be disastrously ready to assume it isn't working, whenever life gets a little rough on them. And they may readily fall into the vices that keep marriage from working: into self-seeking, suspicion, fault-finding, excessive demands, tentative glances elsewhere, all the infidelities of the heart which lead so naturally to infidelity of the body.

It must be admitted that our society rather encourages the vices that lead to adultery. Consider the romantic lie, fostered by many magazines and films and radio programs, that love in the erotic sense is the real meaning of life; that its presence guarantees an effortless and unending happiness; and that its absence means that your marriage is over. Consider the sexual confusion which permits a terrified prudery to rear many of our young people knowing no more of mating than that it is "not nice" — and which combines this ignorance with the constant erotic incitements of our advertising and entertainment. C. S. Lewis again: "We grow up surrounded by propaganda in favor of unchastity. There are people who want to keep our sex instinct inflamed in order to make money out of us. Because, of course, a man with an obsession is a man who has very little sales resistance."

Consider the current psychoanalytic notion that you can't be sane without sex, which impels into ill-starred marriages a good many people who would be much happier celibate. And consider, above all, the tendency to regard marriage *only* as a civil contract — a sort of business deal in which each party should try to get as much and give as little as possible — which each party may feel free to end if the business isn't showing a profit. Marriage cannot live by legality alone, however necessary legality may be. The first consequence of our bit-of-paper morality is a population largely convinced that you are entitled to have anyone you want, as long as by hook or crook you can make it legal. And the second consequence, inevitably, is a widespread conviction that you should have anyone you want, legal or not.

For anyone who thinks at all will soon ask, " How can a bit of paper make adultery right? " And the usual answer is, " It can't; but why is adultery wrong? "

Are we sure that it is wrong, today? Sexual morality has changed a bit since women were set free to earn their own living. For centuries they have suffered in dumb resentment the double standard, explicitly condemned by Christ, which stoned the woman and let the man go unscathed. The true and Christian remedy, obviously, is to hold the men to as high a standard as the women. Finding that impracticable in a man's world, however, many women have concluded that the remedy is to behave as badly as the men; and in an age of birth control and economic freedom they can often get away with it. We've all heard the arguments — something like this: " My self-expression as an individual demands sexual freedom! I am not my husband's property; and I've no intention of presenting him with another man's child to bring up. Why shouldn't I follow love? " Because it is not love; because it is the pursuit of one's own pleasure coupled with a disregard of the needs and emotions of the other people involved; because it begins in self-love and ends in lovelessness. But try to tell them that! You will be informed that you are old-fashioned, Puritanical, and ignorant of modern science.

Other women prefer to punish the men as they could not in the days of woman's dependence; divorcing a husband for adultery is a comparatively modern privilege. The defense of women's rights by our Lord has eventually brought us to a world in which women *have* rights, and are determined to use them. To make marriage last, in the old days, only one person had to be satisfied — the husband. But now two people have to be satisfied, and marriage is correspondingly more unstable.

Half our people are secularists — that is to say, half our marriages are not intended as Christian marriages at all. And the Christians, seeing their neighbors have what seems to be an easier and pleasanter time of it, are tempted to relax their own standards. Hence the slack divorce laws and the casual adulteries. What remedy? Well, first let us eliminate a few remedies that *won't* work. We are not going to get anywhere by a revival of stone-throwing. It should be enough that our Lord commanded, "Judge not." If that is not enough, remember that such episodes as the fuss over the Bergman baby only serve to convince the public that the real principle of sexual morality is, "Don't get caught."

And we are not going to get anywhere by force. All over the world there are well-intentioned clerical politicians trying to write Christian marriage back into the civil statutes — to make the non-Christians of their country live by a religion they do not believe. Two thousand years of failure have not taught some reformers that you can't stop sin by declaring it illegal. Two thousand years have not taught them that you can't save a man's soul by force — you can only lose your own in the attempt. Drunkenness and gambling and secularism and lechery — various hopeful churchmen have earnestly tried to outlaw them all; and what is the result? A drunken nation, a gambling nation, a secularist nation, an adulterous nation. And, often, a ruined Church.

It might be wise, as C. S. Lewis suggests, if we worked instead for "two distinct kinds of marriage: one governed by the State with rules enforced on all citizens, the other governed by the Church with rules enforced by it on its own members." If we are to produce a generation that is *not* blithely adulterous, however, we must start long before marriage — with the young. Education for marriage cannot decently be left, as it is too often left now, in the hands of self-styled marriage counselors, psychological faddists, popular publishing, and popular entertainment. Education for marriage is part of the business of the Church; getting a sane doctrine of sexual relations before the public is a most important task of the Church. The matter cannot safely be left to the State and its schools, for they too are at the mercy of the spirit of the times — and, as Chesterton says in *The Everlasting Man,* "only men to whom the family is sacred will ever have a standard or a status by which to criticize the State."

There is only the Church to teach the young what marriage really means — a union of two into one, not a tentative bargain between warily sparring antagonists. There is only the Church to teach fidelity of body and heart and soul, to remind us that without understanding and honesty and charity any house we build is built on sand. And who but the church can explain *why* adultery is a disaster — can remind us that it is not just a passing physical contact, but a violation of the most tender and sensitive of all relations between human souls?

Meanwhile, let us remember the twin duties of compassion toward others and severity to ourselves. Making our *own* marriages fully Christian is the chief of our tasks. Christian marriage is not easy; Christ never said the Christian life was easy — he came to bring "not . . . peace, but a sword." Yet the Christian form of sexuality is the only form worth having. Either the sexual union is a means toward complete love — a whole-souled joy in which the other becomes the self, an earthly prefiguration of the union with God — or else it is adultery. Let us, then, forget about what we stand to *get* out of marriage and concentrate on what we must *give*. Let us put all our charity and patience and justice and fortitude into our matings, so that they must become true marriages and cannot lapse into adulteries.

VIII

YOU CAN'T CHEAT AN HONEST MAN

Thou shalt not steal. — Ex. 20:15.

YOU ARE a real estate operator in a small Northern city; a prominent citizen, known as a church member, contributor to worthy causes, and esteemed depositor in the local bank. You have just knocked yourself out on a big deal, selling an otherwise unsalable property to an out-of-town man who didn't know the score. You feel entitled to a bit of rest and gaiety in Florida, away from the wife and kiddies. . . .

On the train you somehow fail to put your ticket in the slot provided, and the conductor has to ask you for it. Across the aisle sits a dignified elderly man reading a Church magazine. After the conductor passes, you catch his eye and get into talk. He comes from a little town in your state; he tells you about his Sunday school work, his endeavors against sin. . . . By the time you reach Florida, you and this Mr. Roper are friends and decide to share a hotel room.

One evening, while the two of you are dining, you kick something under the table. It turns out to be a wallet stuffed with currency and stamped with the name of a Mr. O. K. Innside. Roper, fanatic about honesty that he is, finds Innside's name in the hotel register and insists on rushing you up to the fellow's room to return the wallet; rather to your annoyance, Roper will not hear of accepting a reward. But Mr. Innside is grateful, he feels that he must do *something*. He lets you in on a big deal, and you find yourself moving in an undreamed-of world.

Mr. Innside, it appears, works for a syndicate that fixes races. He is here in Florida to lift large quantities of scratch from the local bookmakers, and just out of gratitude he will

95

cut you and Roper in on the deal. Roper is horrified. Racing and gambling are against all his principles. But Mr. Innside points out that since bookies are all crooks, it's a righteous act and a fine moral lesson to separate them from their ill-gotten gains. Pretty soon you find yourself joining with Mr. Innside to talk Roper into spoiling the Egyptians. Eventually, reluctantly, he yields.

In the next few days you visit a bookie joint, you see bets being placed, enormous sums changing hands casually, customers drifting in and out. On tips from Mr. Innside, you win a few hundred yourself. Your head whirls with excitement; when Roper's religious scruples bother him, you cut him short with increasing curtness. Then Innside comes to you with big news; there's a fixed race coming up in which a long shot will pay off at twenty to one.

You rush home. You cash in your Government bonds, you borrow against your stocks, you withdraw your deposits and perhaps even mortgage your house. In a trice you are back in Florida with fifty thousand smackers.

Roper is still uneasy in his conscience, but you and Innside bully him into submission. It's agreed that Roper will place the crucial bet, since you and Innside are now too familiar to the bookie. Skip the details. Roper, whose Sunday school background has unfitted him for distinguishing between win, place, and show, places the bet wrong. You are wiped out. Innside is wiped out. Both of you want to kill Roper. Roper tries to kill himself. Alarmed, you forget your own losses, get a doctor to pump the sleeping pills out of him, and talk him back to sanity. Eventually you find yourself home again in the North, a sadder, poorer, but probably not wiser man.

In the meantime, "Roper," "Innside," the supposed bookie and his clerks, and the supposed customers you saw betting all around you have come together in a tavern and divided your fifty grand.

"I knew the man had larceny in his soul the minute I set eyes on him," says the deacon, alias Mr. Roper. "He was trying to 'ride the plush'—holding his ticket out on the conductor. He won't squawk — too scared the church crowd'll wise up to him."

"Yea, verily," says Mr. Innside with pious unction. "You can't cheat an honest man."

The confidence men are the aristocrats of American crime. They spend like Argentine millionnaires and dress like movie stars; they fix judges, hobnob with legislators, and seldom if ever go to prison; they have been known to buy whole towns, from the mayor down to the cop in the prowl car. No one knows how much of America's income goes annually to keep the con mobs in champagne and blondes, but a single mob operating in Denver was reported to take in about $3,000,000 a year — and that was before the war. And all this incredible wealth and luxury and power derives from one source — the larceny in the souls of the respectable, the eagerness of so many supposedly upright businessmen to steal with both hands the minute they think it's safe.

The Eighth Commandment ought hardly to need reinterpretation. "Thou shalt not steal" means for us exactly what it meant to the ancient Jews — don't take what belongs to the other fellow! Yet some curious confusions have muddled our national attitude to theft. For one thing, the regulations and limits forced upon us by our complex world have muddled our definition of *ownership;* few of us would agree with Proudhon's famous dictum, "Property is theft," yet few of us are quite sure just what property *is.* Certainly we no longer think of it as something a government can't take away whenever it pleases.

And of course the easiest form of theft to recognize is the overt physical act. We can all identify the "strong thief" as a criminal — the mugger, the housebreaker, the safe-cracker, the car stealer, the bank bandit. Nor are we in any doubt as to what is going on if we catch a clerk with his hand in the till, or a bank teller skipping with the cash. But swindling, on the other hand! But rigging contracts, bribing officials, finding loopholes in the tax laws, playing tricks with foreign exchange, lying about the goods we sell and selling trash! How cleverly all these forms of dishonesty can masquerade as legitimate business methods! And how hard it is to detect them — except, perhaps, belatedly and ineffectually, by an occasional investigating committee.

Our society tends to denounce force, particularly when used by the poor, and extenuate fraud, particularly when employed by the rich. Traditional Christians like Dante, who placed the swindlers deeper in hell than the strong-arm men, would disagree with us. Nevertheless we have historical precedent enough; all human societies have done much as we do, and before Christianity they saw nothing amiss in it. The objection to stealing is older than the Ten Commandments, as old as property — but the big question is whether it originated mainly in man's sense of justice or in man's selfishness. At any rate, the "haves" often take it for granted that the laws against theft are directed chiefly at the "have-nots." Consider the Roman law, which crucified a poor thief — and assigned a successful politician a province to be looted for his personal advantage! Consider the Buddhist scripture Anguttara-nikāya, which seeks to show how a man of much virtue may be saved in spite of a misdeed which would send a man of lesser merit to hell, and does so by this bland comparison of the laws of God with those of men:

"Who, O priests, is cast into prison for a halfpenny, for a penny, or for a hundred pence?

"Whenever, O priests, anyone is poor, needy, and indigent: he, O priests, is cast into prison for a halfpenny, for a penny, or for a hundred pence. . . .

"Whenever, O priests, anyone is rich, wealthy, and affluent: he, O priests, is not cast into prison for a halfpenny, for a penny, or for a hundred pence."

And so on and on, with no suggestion that maybe there's something wrong about this state of affairs, O priests!

But the people of the Book knew it was wrong. They interpreted "Thou shalt not steal" in the light of divine justice and not of worldly expediency; the Old Testament, in The Psalms and The Proverbs and the Prophets, condemns the dishonest rich far more strongly than the desperate poor. And no crime in the Bible is held up to more execration than that "due process of law" by which Queen Jezebel murdered Naboth and confiscated his vineyard. The Hebrew teaching on theft reached its culmination when Jesus overturned the tables of the money-changers and labeled these respectable financiers a den of thieves. And this was also he who welcomed the *repentant* thief into paradise.

The Christian definition of theft depends partly on Christ's view of property; and people have been fighting over that ever since Ananias held out a little cash from the common treasury. Socialists of all sorts, even the atheist sort, have seized upon Jesus' contempt for earthly treasure and mammon worship, his treatment of wealth as a curse and sometimes almost a sin — "How hardly shall they that have riches enter into the kingdom of God!" While in the camp of mammon we find such enthusiasts for capitalism as the current publication *Christian Economics,* which proclaims, "We stand for free competitive enterprise," "Profit is essential and Christian," and even, "The only sure way to make money that I know of is to follow the teachings of Jesus." And these too find texts to support them. Perhaps the ultimate depth in this view of Jesus as chief executive assistant to mammon was reached by Bruce Barton's incredible *The Man Nobody Knows,* which justified its portrayal of our Lord as an American big business leader by quoting on the title page, "Wist ye not that I must be about my Father's *business?*"

The extremists of both camps can hardly be interested in Jesus himself at all; they merely find him useful to grind an ax on. They would quote from the devil as readily, had the devil in his own proper person ever written a book. Meanwhile, most Churches have always agreed on a Christian and common-sense view of property, so familiar that we are in danger of forgetting it — property is neither sin nor inalienable right, but a loan, a trust from God. Like the talents in

the parable, it is a test of our faithfulness, and we may keep
it only so long as we use it well. The size of our bank account,
like the size of our biceps, is neither good nor bad in itself,
but only in what we do with it; should we use either money
or muscle wickedly, our fellow men have the duty of stopping
us somehow.

Theft, then, implies depriving a man of property he is *not*
misusing, without making him an adequate return for it. And
most of us would add that theft implies taking property for
an unworthy or selfish motive; thus Robin Hood, though a
thief by legal definition, has never been one to the popular
imagination. We might simplify it by saying that theft is get-
thing something for nothing.

Thus owning capital and employing labor are not theft, unless we fail to treat the laborer as worthy of his hire; thus
making a profit is not theft, unless we make it by usury or
some other form of defrauding others; thus taxation is not
theft, unless the government fails to return to us, in services
and benefits and protection, the equivalent of what it takes
away. And thus, before extending a blanket condemnation or
a blanket approval to any of these three, we had better take
the trouble to find out how they are working in practice.

By a careful definition, the thief is not only he who steals
my purse, but also he who steals my trade; and he who under-
pays me, and he who overcharges me; and he who taxes me
for his own advantage instead of mine; and he who sells me
trash instead of honest goods. The ultimate form of theft,
undoubtedly, is slaveholding, which denies a man even the
ownership of his own body.

It must be admitted that from the beginning Christendom
has gone in for what George Orwell called "doublethink"
about stealing. The Christian view added to its analysis of
property rights a plea for the poor man driven to theft by
want — witness Sir Thomas More in *Utopia:*

"For simple theft is not so great an offense that it ought to
be punished with death. Neither there is any punishment so
horrible that it can keep them from stealing which have no

other craft whereby to get their living. . . . For great and horrible punishments be appointed for thieves, whereas much rather provision should have been made that there were some means whereby they might get their living, so that no one should be driven to this extreme necessity, first to steal, and then to die."

Yes; but meanwhile the governments were putting all their ingenuity into devising "great and horrible punishments" for the penniless thief. The secular law, after all, was based as much on the law of the slaveholding Roman Empire as on the teaching of Christ. Crucifixions, cutting off hands, burnings and boilings and flayings alive, the modern tortures by tear gas and fire hose and solitary cell and psychosurgery — such are always the secular arm's methods of protecting property against the desperate poor. No wonder if this history of cruelty maddened Karl Marx into the wild conclusion that government itself is no more than the self-defense of the rich! And little wonder too if men like Voltaire, seeing these things done in the name of Christ, with the tacit co-operation of a corrupt clergy, could find no better word for the organized religion of their time than "Écrasez l'infâme!"

Yet, wherever faith in Christ was real, it somewhat controlled the misuse of property, if not the punishment of theft. The medieval baron's obligation to his serf was as genuine (in theory, and often in practice too) as the serf's obligation to his baron. The medieval Christian was forbidden to practice usury — he could not lend money at interest, and he might have regarded the modern investment system as the devil's masterwork. The prohibition of usury did indeed disintegrate in the "humanism" of Renaissance Italy; it is no accident that the arms of the neopagan banking house of Medici have become the crest of the modern pawnbroker. What finished the Christian view of property and profit for a while, however, was the early industrial system. As Friedrich Engels remarked, the first capitalists found that "rationalism" served their turn far better than did Christianity with its inconvenient notions about a rich man's duty to his fellows; and for the first time economists and statesmen began to argue that property was not a trust but a sacred right, something with which governments must not meddle. The terrifying strength of Marxism, indeed, springs largely from its revival, for propaganda purposes, of just that part of Christ's teaching about our social responsibility which the nominal Christians of the early nineteenth century did their best to kill.

For the age of capitalism, a hundred years ago, *did* maintain that wealth was both the reward and the proof of virtue, and that money-making methods were something too holy for a government to regulate. The argument reached its logical and ugly conclusion in Negro slavery; both the New England ship captains who traded in slaves and the Southern planters who owned them defended themselves with Old Testament phrases about the sons of Ham being predestined bond servants. So often have ancient Hebrew savageries and crimes been used by certain Protestants to cloak their offenses that one might paraphrase Dr. Johnson by saying that the Old Testament is the last refuge of a scoundrel. It was the Puritan and commercial North that stoned abolitionists and smashed their printing presses. We remember and rightly honor the abolitionist ministers who spoke out against this monstrous perversion of Christianity. But, alas, there were other ministers who spoke on behalf of slavery; have all the reasons of all the atheists ever harmed a church one tenth as much as its own occasional readiness to serve as a den of thieves?

Nowadays some reactionaries talk as if Christ had invented capitalism, and some progressives talk as if modern science had invented Government regulation, and both are talking nonsense. Government regulation of the use and tenure of property is exactly as old as government; indeed, we may question whether, without it, any government could exist at all. " Traditional " laissez-faire capitalism, on the other hand, is a novelty of the last two centuries and a profoundly revolutionary one, somewhat in the spirit of that revolution by which hell hopes to conquer heaven. The problem that most concerns us, however, is not whether a given system is radical or reactionary, but whether it is honest and workable. And perhaps the two adjectives are really one; perhaps a society must be honest in order to be workable. Perhaps a society riddled with theft is inevitably cutting its own throat, for a day must surely come when the victims will have nothing left to steal.

Have we got a society riddled with theft? There are two good places to look for the answer — in the headlines and in our hearts. After the last few years' scandals, we recognize that dishonesty seems to be a commonplace in our political life; and after a brief flurry of indignation we usually accept thieves in high places as inevitable, talk sadly of the decline in national morality, and shrug our shoulders. But do we recognize the thief in the mirror? the dishonesty lurking privately in most of us, without which (if it be true that nations have the governments they deserve) our public dishonesty could hardly exist for long?

A bitter man once said that the great American dream was getting something for nothing.

Grotesque exaggeration this, for we have many better dreams — freedom, equality, the stoic New England tradition of "not being beholden," and the generous idealism which hopes to feed the world. Nevertheless getting something for nothing has insensibly become, for many, the only possible way of making a living. It is not only the unemployed and unemployable who drain a nation's wealth and give nothing in return. All performers of worthless work do that, even if they work themselves to death at it. Think of the armies of Government employees whose function is mainly keeping tabs on the rest of us; the armies of salesmen out plugging junk; the armies of workers madly turning out clothes that disintegrate in the first washing, cars that wear out in the first two years, houses that sag irreparably in the first spring thaw, electric gimmicks to do what a woman would get more fun out of doing herself, electric gadgets that promise a man health without the joy of exercise, amusements that don't amuse, cosmetics that don't beautify, drugs that do not cure,

and education that does not teach — all the hopeless and useless tinsel with which a desperate world tries to bargain for
its daily bread. These armies are not armies of thieves; they
work hard for their keep at the only trades they have been
allowed to learn — "rather provision should have been made
that there were some means whereby they might get their
living."

But a man is subdued to what he works in. The man making
or selling trash eventually realizes it is trash, and loses faith
in his work, himself, and his ethics. In the end he may be like
the shopkeeper who explained business ethics to his son:
"Suppose a customer buys something in a hurry. I give him
change for ten dollars, but the minute he goes out I see he's
given me a hundred-dollar bill by mistake. Now here's the
question of business ethics: should I tell my partner?"

The ultimate stage of a society based on such ethics is col-
lapse — the famous "end of civilization as we know it." And
the penultimate stage is slavery, for when men have nothing
else to lose, they still have their bodies. We have seen a dozen
impoverished nations like Russia and China reach that next-
to-last stage in which men accept slavery in exchange for a
bite of bread. We have seen India driven to live on handouts,
and to obtain handouts with the implied threat of what its
vast man power could do on the Russian side. Our own country still calls itself rich, and still the price of food drives many
to a quiet desperation. Even here, many people feel that their
best hope is to get on the thieves' end of the bargain rather
than the victim's end; to get something for nothing.

The mother who teaches her child to slide under the sub-
way turnstile rather than pay his dime; the athlete who sells
his skill to the highest bidder; the rich man who wins ap-
plause through benevolent foundations that just happen to be
tax-free, and the poor man who feels more comfortable with
Government support than with a job; the bribed policeman
and the bribing bookie, the bribed judge and the bribing
gangster, the bribed Congressman and the bribing industrial-
ist — are they getting something for nothing or aren't they?

And who pays the bill? And what would Christ have called them?

Our society, in some aspects, is a vast confidence game. Even our money sometimes becomes a swindle; no crueler form of theft was ever devised than an inflation, and since the value of paper money depends on that doubtful commodity, faith in the Government, it is hard to see how all present currencies can help inflating. Those who remember the German inflation of the 1920's know what happens, in such cases, to trusting old people living on pensions and savings.

Anyone who promised to cure the ills of our time with easy hopes and facile solutions would be the most heartless of liars. Yet perhaps the world which we all know is nearly bankrupt has just enough time left to stop, and change its mind, and devote the fiery energies it now puts into force and fraud into something new instead — the longed-for just distribution of land and sane production of food. We haven't really much choice in the matter. For either we shall learn to obey " Thou shalt not steal " — which might be rephrased for us as " Thou shalt not try to get something for nothing " — or else we shall be driven to that extreme necessity of which the martyred Thomas More speaks — " first to steal, and then to die."

IX

JESTING PILATE

Thou shalt not bear false witness against thy neighbor.
— Ex. 20:16.

THERE WAS a pious man who said he knew of a plot to over-throw the Government; his conscience made him tell. The plotters he named belonged to a small and already unpopular minority, suspected of taking orders from a foreign power; so he found ready belief. He was believed with especial readiness by certain politicians who had axes of their own to grind and reputable opponents they wanted to discredit.

Our friend proved to have an inexhaustible memory. Each new questioning brought out new facts and new names; Government officials themselves were not above suspicion, and popular hysteria knew no bounds. It seemed you couldn't trust anyone; people you had known and respected for years were ferreted out by the infallible informer, stripped of their livelihood and their freedom. A host of lesser lights sprang up to follow their master in denunciation. Men began to eye their closest friends with suspicion and to look for revolution under the bed at night. The frenzy lasted for several years, during which hard-won civil liberties were cast aside, rules of evidence forgotten, slanders accepted as proof.

The man? One Titus Oates. The year? 1678. The conspiracy? The so-called Popish Plot, which for months had English Protestants believing that their innocent Catholic neighbors were about to murder them with fire and sword.

Of course the seventeenth century was very crude and credulous compared to our enlightened times, in which nothing of the sort could possibly happen. But the seventeenth century had one virtue we should do well to remember. It detested

106

a false witness, once it had caught him. Titus Oates, eventually convicted of his murderous perjuries, was whipped from one end of London to the other.

Indeed there is no human loathing more ancient and innate than our loathing of perjury. Primitive men who killed and raped and looted without a second thought regarded a false oath as an offense against the gods, and looked with superstitious horror for a bolt of lightning to strike the blasphemer dead. The Hebrew Commandment against false witness was itself only a reflection of still older laws. The Babylonian Code of Hammurabi and the Roman laws of the Twelve Tables both agreed that a false witness against a man accused of crime should receive the punishment of that crime. And to Roman law, though not alas to ours, any man who brought about another's execution through giving false evidence was himself guilty of murder. Lies go hand in hand with language, as anyone who has raised a baby knows; yet the chances are that no sooner had the first Neanderthal invented enough words to mouth a calumny than twenty of his fellows invented the words to condemn him with.

"These six things doth the Lord hate; yea, seven are an abomination unto him: a proud look, a lying tongue, and hands that shed innocent blood, a heart that deviseth wicked imaginations, feet that be swift in running to mischief, a false witness that speaketh lies, and he that soweth discord among brethren." The false witness, the wicked heart, the lying tongue, and the troublemaker were early recognized as aspects of the same man and the same sin. A slander shouted in the law court, a slander whispered in the bedchamber, were different only in that the first had the extra crime of oath-breaking on its conscience. Gradually men perceived that there was more than one way to tell a lie and more than one way to hurt your fellows with it. Aleph says, "I saw John kill his wife on the street corner!" Beth says, "I saw John on the street corner!" Gimel won't say anything at all. Yet all three of them have seen John on the corner — and know that he did *not* kill his wife. One lies boldly, one tells an evasive half-truth, one keeps cowardly silence; is there a penny to choose between them? And Daleth the camel dealer, who urges you to buy his swift, strong, young, healthy beast — he means you no harm, he intends only his own gain; but he is hurting you nonetheless, as you find out when you're on the desert far from the oasis and the sick old camel suddenly caves in.

The Hebrews began to feel that there was something a little smelly about *all* tampering with the truth. And when Christ came, his fiercest wrath was for the hypocrite, the living lie whose every action is a false witness to his own virtue. Let us make note of the hypocrite; we shall meet him again, every last one of us, any time we care to look into the mirror. The road to Calvary was lined with many of us whited sepulchers — with scribes who claimed knowledge they had not, and Pharisees who claimed holiness they had not, and false witnesses to identify Christ as a subversive radical, and Judas with his lying kiss. But not until Jesus stood before Pilate was the ultimate lie spoken. What did Pilate mean by his "What is truth?" He seems to have been implying a doctrine fashionable in his time — the lie of the skeptic bound hand and foot in despair, who rather than face his own sins will even doubt his own reality; the question that hints that there is no such thing as truth. We must understand Pilate to understand ourselves, for he may have represented the very modern view that truth is after all a relative and subjective affair, an agreed-upon convention, a matter of expediency — and that therefore we are justified in doing anything that seems expedient, even as Pilate.

Throughout Christian history, denunciations of lying have been loud and frequent. Who has been so abhorred as Ananias? And yet we all know the meaning of the words "pious fraud." From the beginning, the devil has loved to tempt the devout to lie for the sake of their good cause — and thereby make it a bad one. One of the first tasks of the Early Church was to separate the true Gospels from the multitudinous invented "eyewitness" accounts in which the faithful lied their heads off for the supposed good of the Church. Fabulous miracles ascribed to the boy Jesus — and more suitable to an infant devil; romantic adventures of Paul with the holy virgin Thecla; forged donations of Constantine, false Isidorian decretals, profound treatises on metaphysics attributed to a Dionysius the Areopagite who never wrote them but was sainted for them — the list is endless. Nor did it end with antiquity; most modern churches have kept up the good work of forging their own praises and their rivals' dispraise, until that clear-sighted and honest Christian Charles Williams found it necessary to write warningly of " the normal calumnies of piety," and to say of a historian, " In defense of his conclusion he was willing to cheat in the evidence — a habit more usual to religious writers than to historical." Let us clean our own house first.

You can usually tell when a hypocrite has been sinning; he denounces that sin in public — and in somebody else. The mere halfhearted sinner may try to wriggle out of his guilt by some verbal quibble; he hasn't really lied to his wife about how he spent the week end, he just hasn't told her *all* the truth. But the real, thoroughgoing, incarnate lie of a Pharisee covers his guilt by trumpeting loudly about his virtue; he comes forward boldly and denounces *her* for lying to Mrs. Jones about that horrid new hat. And if you want to find a man whose whole life is devoted to hypocritical dishonesty and deception, it might be wise to look for one who habitually beats his child for lying.

As to whether there *is* such a thing as a white lie — well, no one has yet devised a rule of conduct that can be applied to every imaginable case, and the rule against lying is no exception. Here, as elsewhere, charity and common sense must be our guides. If a man comes to my door waving a gun and announcing that he'll shoot his wife the minute he finds her, I shall certainly tell him I have not seen her for a week, even though I've just finished hiding the poor woman in my closet. And it would be an uncharitable sort of truthfulness that, when asked, told a doting mother exactly what it thought of her small son's fiddle-playing. All the same, it is possible that most of our white lies are told, not for charity, but for laziness and for cowardice — to save the work of thinking up a real answer, or to avoid a trivial social discomfort.

The great problem, however, is not the reluctant occasional social lie, but the habitual and automatic lie — the false witness borne unblushingly for personal advantage, until lying becomes a way of life. How does a baby grow up into a Titus Oates?

No doubt he begins to learn in infancy. Suppose little Titus, age four, tries to lie himself out of a scrape. He is rebuked with horror by a self-righteous parent; but the horror, let us assume, arises less from outraged principle than from the selfish desire to keep Titus under the fatherly thumb. As C. S. Lewis has pointed out, parents and schoolmasters object to the lie partly because it is "the only defensive weapon of the child." And Titus' father tells a few whoppers himself. He threatens that the tongue of Titus will shrivel up, the lips of Titus will be sewn together by the devil's darning needle; he pretends that he can tell, by a single penetrating parental glance, whether Titus is truthful.

Nothing outrages our vanity so much as being seen through by our own children; and yet see through us they must, if they are ever to find their own way through the world. Soon enough Titus will know that Father too is a liar. Father lies about sex and his own sexual behavior, money and his own way of making it, his own importance, and his own holiness. Titus concludes that the lie is the way of the world; and that the people who take what you say at its face value are only children and fools, meant by nature to be deceived.

In abandoning the traditional penalties for a false witness, modern law courts may perhaps be guided by the policeman's natural longing to have a stool pigeon do his work for him; and the prosecutor's eagerness to build a career on buried men's bones; and most of all, perhaps, by the political usefulness of the frame-up. It is *still* expedient that one man die for the people. But law courts like that argue a society gone rotten, a society that (like Pilate's Rome, with its smattering

of Greek philosophy) has lost not only its respect for truth
but even its power of defining truth.

"'What is truth?' said jesting Pilate; and would not stay for
an answer." Perhaps we do Pilate an injustice; perhaps, under
the fashionable skepticism of the Roman gentleman, he really
wanted to know. And perhaps what unsettles the modern
mind most is its despair of ever knowing truth amid the conflicting and untrustworthy and very dusty answers we get in
our daily life. There are people who believe that not only are
there no truths, but there are not even facts — all is a matter
of "subjective values." Whatever the merits of this as philosophy, its practical use is often as a method of evasion and
rationalization, a means to the loss of faith and the loss of
honor. We have all heard the arguer who, driven into a corner
by relentless proof, slips away with an easy, "Oh, well, it's
all in how you think of it, isn't it?"

The denial that truth exists is a good beginning for habitual
lying. And if we start confessing our habitual lies, shall we
ever be done? There are the lies of gossip, public and private,
which make haters out of us; the lies of advertising and sales-
manship, which make money out of us; the lies of politicians,
who make power out of us. And the lies of the sort of
journalist who manufactures a daily omniscience out of the
teletype machine and the *Encyclopædia Britannnica!* And the
lies of a professional patriot who assures us that our cause is
so just that it doesn't matter what injustice we commit
in its name! Two hundred years ago Dr. Johnson wrote:

"Among the calamities of war may be justly numbered the
diminution of the love of truth by the falsehoods which interest dictates and credulity encourages. A peace will equally
leave the warrior and the relater of wars destitute of employ-
ment; and I know not whether more is to be dreaded from
streets filled with soldiers accustomed to plunder or from
garrets filled with scribblers accustomed to lie."

The observation still holds good, except that the scribblers
no longer live in garrets. The pay is bigger nowadays — but
then, so are the lies.

Greatest and first of a man's lies are usually those he tells about himself. Hitler could not have forced the "big lie" technique down the throat of Germany if he had not begun by lying about the goodness and wisdom of Hitler. Stalin could hardly have been cynical about *Pravda's* misrepresentation of the United States, if he had not earlier grown cynical about Stalin's misrepresentation of Stalin. Well for us if only great men could be great hypocrites, but unfortunately this sort of greatness is possible to us all. Our world has no more typical false witness than the false expert, who makes a career by pretending omniscience about some recondite and perhaps illusory subject — from the stars' influence on our destinies to the stars we want to see in the movies next year. And this sort of lying is always "against our neighbor," for such expert knowledge is advanced as a means to power or profit. Stalin's supposed science of history somehow led to the conclusion that Stalin should have absolute rule; and what the astrologer sees in the stars has a way of lining the pockets of the astrologer.

But we are not such as these, are we? We are not crooked politicians or fake fortune tellers or pseudo experts; even in business we hardly ever tamper with the truth for our own advantage.

And yet it is still possible that we tell the most fundamental of lies — that we lie to ourselves about ourselves. Not for profit or power; but for pride. It is possible that, in the secret places of our minds, we deny our sins.

Some may argue that we are honestly unconscious of our sins; that is, that the hypocrite is essentially a truthful man because he is self-deceived into believing what he says. The unconscious mind is a favorite modern scapegoat; whatever may *really* be in it, many of us have mastered the trick of excusing, as "unconscious drives," behavior whose true motives we know only too well. No doubt we often bewilder ourselves successfully about our motives. Yet we *can* usually tell when we have "done those things which we ought not to have done," or "left undone those things which we ought to have done." And unless we face the truth about that, we are lost.

For the only way to get rid of a sin is to admit it. Without honesty, repentance and forgiveness and grace are not possible. Nowadays the conviction of sin is widely misunderstood — secularists pity Christians, whom they picture as men bowed to the ground under an enormous burden of self-condemnation, men who go around all the time feeling guilty. Actually, of course, as anyone who has experienced conversion knows, the Christian is the only man who does *not* go around all the time feeling guilty. For him, sin is a burden he can lay down; he can admit, repent, and be forgiven. It is the unfortunate creature who denies the existence of sin in general, or his own in particular, who must go on carrying it forever.

Alas, it is dreadfully easy for a man to lie to himself about his own offenses; that is why Christendom has always approved confessing them to somebody else. And that particular sort of lie becomes a habit more readily than any other. Where does the conscious inner rationalization pass into the unconscious defense mechanism; the willed hypocrisy pass into the unwilled delusion? That is, where is the dividing line between sane lying and insanity? No matter how hard our courts and our committees try to decide that, they can never be quite sure. Perhaps many of the false witnesses end by crossing the dividing line and believing their own tales. We cannot say, nor should we presume to say; for judging other men's hearts is not *our* business. But there is one man most of us can be reasonably sure about — the man in the mirror. We do have the job of looking inward and facing the unpleasant truthful witness of our consciences.

The alternative is a horrible one, beginning and ending in pride. At first we may lie about our virtues; we progress to lying about our deserts; in a moment more, we lie about the world's reasons for denying us the good things we so obviously deserve; and ultimately we may feel justified in telling any lie to get those good things — a woman, a job, a victory, or only a moment of safety. Nor can we escape these peripheral lies as long as we cling to the great central lie of the self. The way to freedom, however, was shown us long ago; it consists in the honest confession and repentance that alone can open our hearts to the Comforter:

" Even the Spirit of truth; whom the world cannot receive, because it seeth him not, neither knoweth him: but ye know him; for he dwelleth with you, and shall be in you."

X

THE MOTH AND THE RUST

Thou shalt not covet thy neighbor's house, thou shalt not covet thy neighbor's wife, nor his manservant, nor his maidservant, nor his ox, nor his ass, nor any thing that is thy neighbor's.
— Ex. 20:17.

ONCE THERE WAS a boy named James Watt, and he had an old teakettle that belonged to his mother. And one day, behold, a great hissing cloud, and a vague shape that said: "I am the genie Steam; and I serve the owner of the teakettle. What is your will, O Master?"

And the boy said: "Make us all rich. Bring us miles of woven cloth, and piles of food, and acres of diamonds; let us have houses that touch the sky and coaches that run swifter than the wind, and let all this be done without our having to strain ourselves with overwork."

"To hear is to obey, Master!" answered the genie. And in the twinkling of an eye all men became rich and happy, neither did they study war any more, but spent their time contentedly enjoying the flow of good things provided by the genie of the kettle. . . .

Or so the dream ran, for its first dreamers. Since then we have extended it somewhat. We have sent the genie for his swifter brother Petroleum, and then for his tall, glittering sister Electricity, and we have put all three to work turning out riches for us, until every man of us has become entirely happy and peaceful. . . . Well, perhaps not quite. But now we have learned to call up the great-granddaddy of all genies, the towering cloud-and-fire shape named Atomic Power, and by his efforts we are certain to content all our desires at last. . . .

115

Well, perhaps not quite.

Yet it was a good and hopeful dream when it started. Ancient and medieval men talked of a golden age in the past, a reign of Saturn or a Garden of Eden, lost beyond recapture; and they shrugged wistfully, and turned again to face the bitter present and the dark future. Modern men, however, have for two hundred years or so looked for the earthly paradise *ahead* of them. Utopia is for them no longer the Land of Nowhere, but the Land of Somewhen; no longer a consoling daydream of escape, but a practical possibility. With power and machines, one could stuff every man's belly with chicken, drape every woman's shoulders with silk, fill every child's heart with laughter. And since one could, one should. The march to the earthly paradise became a new moral absolute and a new religion, under the name of progress.

Let no one say that the dream was a dream of sefishness. The first machine makers lived in a time of revolutionary ferment, when the rights of man were on everybody's lips. When Blake swore to build Jerusalem " in England's green and pleasant land," he was moved not by greed but by Christian compassion for the suffering poor and by white-hot Christian anger at injustice. When Jefferson declared that " life, liberty and the pursuit of happiness," were " unalienable rights," he did so at some risk to the life, liberty, and happiness of Thomas Jefferson. Both Christian charity and secular deism combined to want an end of such miseries as Hogarth painted in *Gin Lane;* the poet and clergyman Cartwright, who invented the power loom, did so out of pity for the endless crippling labor of the hand weaver. He could not have expected that in a few years weavers would be smashing and burning his machines as a cause of their unemployment. For greed came in, soon enough; the men who looked a hundred years ahead were as always easily victimized by the men who looked only to their pockets; the profiteer who can himself dream of nothing but money is quick to cash in on the dreams of better men. Nevertheless it was a noble thing, that early vision of a Kingdom of God on earth in which, since every man would have whatever he needed, no man could be driven to covetousness.

At first, too, progress looked so easy! One didn't have to work at achieving the Kingdom, for it was coming of itself. Just let us alone, said the laissez-faire capitalists, and our enlightened self-interest will enrich the world. The machine smashers, the union agitators of early days, may have been hanged and transported so savagely, not as radicals, but as reactionaries: traitors to the new hope of all mankind. Fifty years soberer, however, the thinkers learned from the horrors of child labor and mine murder that the Kingdom could not be achieved so simply; that progress required more than profit making: it required conscience and regulation and taking thought and working hard. The great humanitarian movements of the nineteenth century were born. Dickens wrote against prisons and slums, Lincoln freed the slaves, the English Fabian Society campaigned for an ideal socialism to be reached an inch at a time. Another fifty years, and patience ran out. The desperate nations of Europe turned from progress by reform to the Fascist and Communist gospel of progress by violence; one must achieve the earthly paradise instantly, at all costs, or it would be too late. Yet, though the ritual has changed so much in these years, the goal has not changed at all. The goal is still material plenty for everybody; and the hope is still that men who are rich enough will become, somehow, just, peaceful, and loving men.

In the moment before waking, dreams sometimes change to nightmares. And in the nightmarish last minutes of the progress dream, we often forget how good it was for a while. We talk as if all Western civilization since the Renaissance were no more than a sinful mistake, as if technical advances had never given us anything but shoddy goods and greedy hearts. Yet much was accomplished by the belief in progress and much more by the striving for it; to give one instance, mothers no longer have to bear ten children in the hope of raising two.

To some extent we in America *have* realized the dream. We

are richer than any previous nation, well fed and well clothed to the point of wastefulness; where a medieval woman kept a dress for a lifetime, our girls throw it away in a year because it's out of style, and where bygone Frenchwomen devised a nourishing soup from an end of cheese, a crust of bread, half an onion, and some leftover meat broth, all many of us can think of when we see such is a quick trip to the garbage can. And we are safer than any previous nation, safe to the point of softness; we fret about muggers on city streets, juvenile delinquents, corrupt politicians, and explain all these as "psychopathic"—but to our ancestors dangerous streets and violent youth and wicked rulers were merely the normal hazards of life. And we live longer, healthier, better-insured lives than the men of previous nations. As far as material goods go, our earthly paradise has given us more, far more, than the first progress worshipers ever dreamed possible.

Yet there is one indispensable condition of paradise lacking. We are not happy in the place. Nor, for that matter, can we honestly maintain that we are completely just and peaceful and loving in it.

The nations of Europe have some time ago wakened screaming from their dream. We are still lulled by comfort, but even so we are beginning to echo their wail: something has gone wrong, the world is in crisis, and all our attempts to struggle out of the quicksands of this life have only gotten us deeper in. In short, the richer we are, the worse off we seem to be. Many explanations of the world crisis have been offered—technological unemployment, wrong distribution of the wealth, overpopulation with its consequent exhaustion of the farm land. No doubt all have some truth in them, particularly as applied to the poorer countries. But none of them will do adequately for us. We have solved technological unemployment by constantly increasing production until now we have to employ women as well as men; we are solving distribution with taxes and Government services; we look to solve the food shortage with conservation and scientific agriculture. Meanwhile we're comfortable enough. Yet who would dare to tell contemporary

America that it is rejoicing in an unparalleled golden age? We manage to be restless and discontented. Why?

Perhaps we had better look beyond the explanations, at the dream itself. Perhaps it was the wrong dream. Perhaps, in spite of its apparent nobility and charity, something is false in the doctrine that you can make men happy and virtuous by making them rich?

We have planned for the more abundant life; we have exalted free competition, i.e., the desire to get more of the world's rewards than our neighbor; we have declared (to quote D. R. Davies' provocative *The Sin of Our Age*) that " the good life has become inseparable from the maximum possible consumption of things. . . . The dogma of the new religion is the dogma of increasing wants." Can we reasonably expect happiness from an insatiable appetite which, no matter how it stuffs its belly, is still psychologically like Oliver Twist in the poorhouse, holding up an empty bowl and begging, " I want some more "? Isn't it possible that our dream of the good society contained, from the beginning, a hidden violation of the Tenth Commandment — " Thou shalt not covet thy neighbor's goods "?

If worldly plenty could stop coveting, the ancient Jews might not have needed the Tenth Commandment. " Surely the land floweth with milk and honey," said the explorers, bringing figs and pomegranates and a great bunch of grapes that took two men to carry. We hear of the corn and wine, of the flocks of sheep and the wild deer of the mountains, of myrrh and frankincense and lilies and cedars — " a fountain of gardens, a well of living water, and streams from Lebanon." This is scarcely fable; Israel in those days was a green and flowery pleasance that needed no reclaiming. Before two thousand years of wasteful agriculture did their work, the whole Mediterranean basin overflowed with milk and honey; Greece was fruitful and southern Italy luxuriant, the coast of North Africa blossomed with garden cities, and Egypt was the granary of Rome. Whenever the spirit seized him, a man might retire into the wilderness to commune with God, and live not too badly for years on whatever came his way. Today, in the same wilderness, he would die in a week.

Only those who burst into our prairies, and stared at the great buffalo herds and the clouds of passenger pigeons, have ever in modern times seen anything like the abundance of that ancient world. Every great nation of antiquity had reason to dream of happiness-through-wealth — the Athenians with their silver mines and ships, the princes of Hind with their gold and elephants, the Romans with their empire. And all alike found that some perversity of human nature defeated the dream. For men coveted. Men found themselves hankering after their neighbor's ox or slave – or even his wife; no oversupply of women ever prevented *that*. No matter how many fat sheep the rich man had, it was always the poor man's ewe lamb that caught his eye. No one who had once learned to identify happiness with wealth ever felt that he had wealth enough.

The nations looked at the state of soul called covetousness, and recognized it as an ugly, itching misery; a destroyer of men and ruiner of the state; an enemy to all joy — in short, a sin. Their chance of escaping it, however, was limited by their degree of insight. The crystalline Greek mind gave us Aesop's fable of the envious and covetous man to whom Zeus granted any wish he liked on condition that his neighbor would get twice as much of it; unable to bear the thought of another's luck, he wished to lose one eye! The Greeks gave us, too, the reverse of the coin, the story of rich King Croesus wallowing in his gold, beside himself with mortification because he could not make the Athenian philosopher Solon envy him. But the Greek moral was only that earthly prosperity is insecure — "Call no man fortunate until he is dead." India, where greed and gold were at their worst, reacted more violently — to extremes of asceticism which thought the only alternative to wanting everything at all costs was wanting nothing at any price. And Eastern "nonattachment" does have the advantage of rescuing men from slavery to their appetites and their envies; yet wanting nothing, when carried to extremes, leaves us not wanting help, not wanting love, not wanting God — and the name of such self-sufficiency is pride. When the Roman Stoics took up nonattachment, they did so with a far too keen sense of their superiority to their unstoical neighbors.

The pagans could see that desiring wealth made you miserable and getting it did not make you happy. But they seem to have had little else to offer, except a sort of gloomy snobbery which felt itself too good for the good things of this world. The Jews saw more clearly, for they recognized that the gifts of God are worth having, but forbade men to desire them *in the wrong way*.

The Tenth Commandment is unique; its predecessors deal with specific actions, but this alone forbids a state of mind. It is the first implied awareness that wrong ideas precede wrong actions, and that no matter how pious and decorous a man's outward behavior may be, if he encourages his mind to seethe with hate and greed he is an abomination in the sight of God. It may be, indeed, that this Commandment comes last because it represents a transition from the old idea of a God who is bound by the physical actions of a prescribed ritual to the new awareness of a God who is spirit, and looks beyond all actions to the heart. Yet the transition is not complete. The counsel remains negative: it forbids coveting but it does not tell a man what he should do instead. And, with the characteristic limitation of Judaism, it assumes that virtue can be achieved by will power alone — that a man is the master of his own house and can feel what emotions he likes. The Tenth Commandment does not tell us *how* to stop coveting.

Not until Christ came were we shown the real alternative to covetousness, in that charity which not only loves to give but also takes with love. And not until Paul taught us did we understand how a man may appeal to the Grace for help against the covetousness in his own heart.

Christianity is everywhere paradoxical, everywhere too difficult for simple black-and-white thinking; but nowhere more so than in its doctrine of worldly goods. For they *are* good things — and yet we must not long for them. They *are* to be enjoyed — and yet we must not make that enjoyment our goal.

They are God's plenty; in the form of bread and wine, they are the very symbols of that act of God which makes and keeps us man; they are " things ye have need of," yet we must not devote our lives to getting them. If we have them, the best possible thing we can do is to give them away; if we don't have them, we may expect to get them, but we mustn't worry about it! The Saviour who bestows miraculous loaves and fishes upon the multitude is the same who proclaims that man does not live by bread alone, and he who teaches us to pray, " Give us this day our daily bread," also warns us, " Take no thought, saying, What shall we eat? " It seems almost that we are told not to desire what, by our very natures, we cannot live without.

The paradox is easier once we remember that the text runs, " Seek ye *first* the kingdom of God " — once we remember the distinction between ends and means. Seeing God face to face is our goal; the pleasures of life, and even life itself, are the means to it. Therefore the milk and honey and corn and wine and soft chairs and fine houses and swift automobiles — all those pleasant things! — exist primarily as a kind of currency of love; a means whereby men can exchange love with one another and thus become capable of the love of God.

In charity, we value such things not only for their pleasantness, but also because we can give them away and give our love with them; or else because, in receiving them, we receive others' love for us as a baby at the breast sucks his mother's love with her milk. Nowadays we usually praise the power to give, which implies worldly success, far beyond the power to take, and we are sometimes ashamed of " receiving charity." Yet Christ and the apostles were not. Though it be more blessed to give than to receive, to be fully Christian one must know how to do both with the same humility and the same joy.

Do we then, if we are covetous, value our earthly treasures for their pleasantness alone? No such luck. The covetous man may begin with that, and at least there is some delight in it, something that comes from God. But he doesn't keep it long. " Covetousness, which is idolatry! " said Saint Paul. Almost at once the coveter makes a god of his possessions, asks more than pleasure from them, asks that serenity of soul which only God can give. And Saint Paul might have said, "Covetousness, which is hate." For the man soon learns to value what he gets chiefly because his fellows can't have it; to desire his neighbor's wife, not because she is beautiful, but because she is another's. And Paul might have ended with, "Covetousness, which is pride." Before long the gold and elephants, the convertibles and chinchillas, are no use at all to the coveter in themselves; he will drop them the instant they go out of fashion, he even resents them a little as responsibilities; but he must have them to convince himself that he is all-powerful, all-successful, all-important — in fact, God. For a while he may tolerate the existence of his neighbors, since it reassures him to have somebody around to envy him; but in the end he will covet their very lives, for he cannot be satisfied as long as anything exists in all eternity that he does not possess. A thousand sayings in a hundred languages testify to the insatiability of covetousness — "He will never have enough," goes the grim Scottish proverb, "till his mouth is filled with mold."

So much, the Christian world has always known. How it has *lived* is another story. Almost from the beginning men wanted the Church to be a strong organization, and then saw that it would be stronger if it could grow rich. An order of friars would be founded dedicated to poverty — and would end by owning half the countryside. The temptation was very natural. But the Middle Ages did at least know that it was a temptation; did at least reject covetousness in theory and regard poverty as a necessary part of holiness. The medieval ideal reached its highest expression, perhaps, when Saint Francis married the Lady Poverty and found the marriage a happy one, with meat enough on the table and plenty of singing.

Nowadays we think very differently. Few of us, whether Christian or secularist, can imagine that a sane man would voluntarily *seek* poverty; and where the old theologians talked of the self-mortification of the ascetic, the modern psychiatrist talks of the guilt complex of the religious maniac. In the nineteenth century, some pious money-makers argued that wealth was God's reward of their virtue, and that therefore a poor man had no right to be angry. But today our materialist reformers seem to argue that wealth *is* virtue, and that therefore a poor man has no right to be happy! Our usual snap judgment, if we see hillbillies managing to live contentedly without electricity and plumbing, is, " They don't know any better."

To make matters worse, we are most of us underprivileged in our own eyes. Let Davies speak again: " Poverty has been promoted to be the chief evil of human existence. . . . Men can no longer be judged to be poor by what they consume, but by what they think they should consume, and do not. . . . Even though their bellies be bursting with chicken, the vast majority of people would still be poor if a minority of bellies were bursting with turkey."

Yet there is a good Christian reason for our changed view. The poverty of medieval days, of an agricultural world short on manufactures but long on food and fuel, was often a tolerable and even a cheerful condition; but the poverty of the modern industrial slum is very different. No one who has seen a mining town when the mine shuts down can seriously argue that it is not the duty of all Christians to end poverty like *that*. Indeed the great ethical contribution of our age is its sensitive social conscience, for we are almost the first of men to understand that all men's welfare is our business. We are the first who blame ourselves when a million Chinese starve; who consider it our task, as the scoffer said, to provide Hottentots with milk; the first, perhaps, since Christ himself and his immediate followers, who have said and really *meant:* One world, one race of man.

Many Christians, though keenly sensitive to the dangers of greed and discontent that come with an economy of continually increasing consumption, nevertheless feel that it is worth risking if only it can end man's physical miseries. The trouble is that it can't. In a finite world, continually increasing consumption is just not possible. Some modern fabulist once put this very neatly; he wrote of a wonderful atomic converter which took common earth and stone and turned out whatever goods you wanted. Men rejoiced at the end of all poverty and laughed at the few reactionaries who feared that the world might get used up. Five thousand years later, astronomers were disproving with mathematics the popular legend that the earth had once been much bigger than the moon. Ten thousand years later the story ended — with one starving ancient, perched on his converter, adrift in empty space.

One need not labor the point. We all know there's a world food shortage; that our scientists are developing ways of feeding pigs on urea, cattle on cactus, and men on seaweed; that even in our own rich land the price of meat often seems rather odd. We have seen the vision of space flight grow in one generation into a serious project, as our necessities force us to seek arable land on the unknown stars. We find ourselves constrained to keep poorer nations alive on our dwindling surpluses, partly through charity but also partly through fear lest they unite with our enemies and take our wealth by force. As always with the treasures of this world, moth and rust corrupt and thieves break through and steal. Our idolatry of worldly goods in which we trusted — was it only covetousness at bottom, after all?

Can the best of us feel sure that he is not corrupted by "the dogma of increasing wants"? Most of us are modest enough in our demands. We reject the disease of greed, the perversion that turns a decent little shopkeeper into a recluse dead of hunger on a mattress stuffed with ten-dollar bills; turns a cheerful girl in a shabby coat into a fretful neurotic in diamonds and mink; turns an idealistic young writer into a twitching Hollywood executive out to knife his best friend in the back. These, we feel, are exceptions and mental cases. *We* could never go like that. We don't grudge our neighbor any success; we just want a standard of living that will enable us to maintain our self-respect. We've no heart's desire for a Cadillac — we'll be satisfied with a Chevvy, for this year at least; and of course we've got to buy a television set, but that's only because the kids are so humiliated on account of all their friends' already having one. . . .

Waking from our dream of plenty into hungry daylight, we turn back to God. The lapsed Christians and the lifelong secularists are beginning to recognize that only the Almighty can untangle the snarl of this world; are coming back into the churches and humbling themselves in prayer. So far so good. But for what do we pray? Do we "cry to dream again"? Do we ask the Lord, not for heaven, but for a way of keeping the automobiles and the television sets?

A certain rich man, we are told, came to Christ and asked to be accepted as a disciple. He was a good and generous and law-abiding youth; yet our Lord asked one thing more of him — "Sell all thou hast, and give to the poor." And the rich man "went away sorrowful: for he had great possessions."

That is exactly our case. We sometimes come to God, not because we love him best, but because we love our possessions best; we ask Christ to "save Western civilization," without asking ourselves whether it is entirely a civilization that a Christian could want to save. We pray, too often, not to do God's will, but to enlist God's assistance in maintaining our "continually increasing consumption." And yet, though Christ promised that God would feed us, he never promised that God would stuff us to bursting.

What, then, must we pray for? Nothing that we have not been told over and over again; nothing but "Thy will be done," even if his will is that we lose all that the last two hundred years have given us. We must pray to face our fear honestly. There is no use pretending that our elaborate technology *can't* be destroyed; like all other civilizations, it can. There is even less sense in pretending that we can't live without it; we can, as men did before it was dreamed of. Let us pray to be free of the idolatry of material things, and then at least we may be able to enjoy them when we have them, instead of being enslaved by them and by the fear of losing them. Our best wisdom may indeed ask God to save our way of life, but his wisdom might conceivably conclude that our way of life is too rich for our blood, that what we need is a purge. At the moment we are still often seeking God not for himself but so that we can hire him as night watchman to mammon. But if we seek him indeed, we shall find that going to church and praying are only the beginning, that our whole lives change from the heart outward until we are no longer interested in mammon. There is, in the last analysis, only one way to stop covetousness and the destruction of body and soul that spring from covetousness, and that is to want God so much that we can't be bothered with inordinate wants for anything else.

XI

LIGHT OF LIGHT

*Jesus said unto him, Thou shalt love the Lord thy God with
all thy heart, and with all thy soul, and with all thy mind. This
is the first and great commandment. And the second is like
unto it, Thou shalt love thy neighbor as thyself. On these two
commandments hang all the law and the prophets.*
— Matt. 22:37–40.

THE TELEPHONE rings. It *would* ring, of course, just when
your typewriter is at last clacking happily; an article that has
been agonizingly slow to start is finally under way. Mutter-
ing something censorable, you break off in the middle of a
sentence and go to answer the ring. Perhaps, at least, the
interruption will be a pleasant one?

No such luck. The caller is a neighbor who is well established as the neighborhood nuisance; a bitter, malicious old
woman who has divorced her husband, driven away her children, quarreled with her friends, and walked out of her
church — and who is now eating her unrepentant soul out in
loneliness and self-pity. You're the only one for miles who
still speaks to her, and you don't enjoy doing it. Today she
says, with a consciously pathetic catch in her voice, that she's
absolutely desperate, and won't you come over and cheer her
up?

Rebellion surges in your mind. Oh, no, not again! You think
in a flash of all the times you've tried in vain to tell her of
God and repentance and grace, only to be jeered at as a
credulous fool. You think of the good practical advice scorned,
the attempts at reassurance sneered at. You know very well
that this time too all you will get from her will be a denunciation of other people, an assertion of her own perfect virtue,

and a series of small nasty digs at yourself. But not this time, not just as you've finally managed to get started writing — it's too much. After all, one can't help those who don't really *want* to be helped.

You open your mouth to tell her, "Sorry, I can't come today, because I'm writing an article about Christ's commandment to love your neighbor —"

Oh, well. You gulp. You say, "Be right over," and, with a last sad look at your typewriter, off you go.

That is what happened to this article half an hour ago; not that the writer is ordinarily so mindful of Christian duties, but because in this case the reminder was sharp enough to penetrate the densest Christian. Right here the article breaks off, and will be resumed after some attempt has been made to love a neighbor.

. . . Well, you come back. You *did* cheer her up a little, after all. You're not any too cheerful yourself, thinking of your wasted working hours and your vanished good ideas and the old lady's poisoned darts still sticking to your hide. Nevertheless, deep inside you, there is a small bright glow.

It's an unreasonable feeling. From the practical point of view you've thrown away a day — a bit of your life — and got nothing in exchange for it. From the practical point of view some of your inalienable rights have been alienated, and you ought to be feeling injured and cheated — pretty much as the old lady usually feels, in fact. Yet the small miraculous happiness persists. Everything in your education, in the modern climate of opinion, urges you to reject it as "merely subjective." It's not real, not valuable; it's only vanity, or only sentimentality; it won't get you one step nearer to worldly success. Perhaps you are even half ashamed of it, and you may try to push it away.

Don't. It will vanish soon enough in any case; your self will descend like a wet blanket and put the glow out. But while it lasts, take a good look at the brightness and recognize it for the love of God. Your love for him and his for you; the realest thing you have even experienced, sweeter than wine and brighter than the sun. For one moment you forget the self and its desires and its rights; you gave a scrap of your life away, and in return you get this incredible candle in the heart for a moment.

What if the candle never went out, but spread and strengthened and filled your whole consciousness forever? What new and miraculous life might you hope to get, if you ever managed to throw your life away entirely?

That is what Christ told us to try for — the full blaze of God's love, inexpressible delight of soul and body, joy beyond all joys. That is what we were put into the world to find; and the world itself, seen clearly, exists primarily to help us to find it, as a hothouse to nurse our growing spirits along until they are strong enough for the unimaginable outdoors we call heaven. That is the reward of our virtue. So we must believe, if we believe that Christ was the incarnate God and that his promises will be kept.

And so we do believe, quite sincerely on the whole, we churchgoers — with our lips and with our minds, for an hour or so on Sundays and five minutes or so at our daily prayers and whatever other time we happen to think about it. Yet the real test of belief is action. A man might assure us quite sincerely that he had no superstitions, and leave us unconvinced if we saw him hastily cross the street to avoid a black cat. Similarly, we know we believe that two and two make four, because we're willing to pay our bills on the strength of our addition; we know we have faith in electricity, because we are willing to trust it to run our houses. By that test, how many of us have enough belief in the love of God to trust it to run our lives?

How often we have heard that virtue is its own reward! By now we can scarcely hear it seriously at all; we make the cynical misinterpretation that there *is* no reward for virtue. For a long while we have thought of virtue negatively, as a saying *no* to various temptations, and the very word has come to have grim and joyless overtones. It seldom occurs to us that virtue might be a pleasure — that it is its own reward because

no other reward could be so nice; that virtue is the state of
mind in which the love of God can really be enjoyed.

In short, we have accepted the prohibitive Ten Commandments, in the sweat of our brows and the sorrow of our hearts.
But the joyous, liberating commandments of Christ we have
yet to learn.

And we fear that if we give up the self nothing will be left
of us but a dry, empty husk like a dead snail shell. It seldom
occurs to us that the Holy Spirit is only waiting till the self
is out — waiting to rush in and fill us with luminous splendors.
Throwing away the self is like squeezing the water out of a
half-drowned man's lungs, not because you want his lungs
empty but because you want the air to get in so that he can
live. For the self is asphyxiating and killing us; the only air
we are designed to breathe is God.

What ails us? We know all this; we've been told it a
thousand times. Yet how many of us actually live on the
assumption that the whole business of life is getting to heaven?

What has made both God and heaven seem a little unreal
to many moderns, who nevertheless think of themselves as
religious men? Pride, partly, which makes us want to be
virtuous without God's help, and respectability, partly, which
makes us distrust any enthusiasm strong enough to be un-
dignified, even an enthusiasm for God. But mostly the materialist climate of opinion in which we live. To materialism,
things are real only if you can perceive and measure them;
thus, for instance, a man's thoughts are somehow less real
than the block of metal he is thinking about, even if his
thoughts show him how to blow that block of metal into
electronic smithereens. And popular misunderstanding often
confuses *real* with *solid* — thus many people found it hard to
believe in electricity and radioactivity until they saw what
these impalpable forces could do to solid objects. The first
men who defined God as a spirit without body, parts, or passions, must have thought of spirit as stronger and more
significant than matter, must have pictured a living Light in
which body and parts and passions could only make dark

holes. But we have been trained to think the other way, and are more likely to picture a dead darkness lacking everything that means existence. To put it bluntly: will the average American high school graduate easily believe that a God who is not solid and measurable can nevertheless deliver more horsepower than the most thoroughly souped-up hot rod? Or does he think it indecent to imagine God delivering horse-power at all?

For many contemporaries God has dwindled into a noble abstraction, a tendency of history, a goal of evolution; has thinned out into a concept useful for organizing world peace — a good thing as an idea. But not the Word made flesh, who died for us and rose again from the dead. Not a Personality that a man can feel any love for. And not, certainly, the eternal Lover who took the initiative and fell in love with *us*.

Is it shocking to think of God as a pursuing lover? Then Christianity is shocking. If we accept the supernatural only as something too weak and passive to interfere with the natural, we had best call ourselves materialists and be done with it — we shall gain in honesty what we lose in respect-ability. Here's a test to tell if your faith is anything more than faith-and-water. Suppose that tonight the Holy Spirit lifts you high into space, speaks a message to your conscience, then invisibly tucks you back into your safe little bed again. Will you consider the possibility that this experience is genuine? Or will you conclude at once that you must be crazy, and start yelling for a psychiatrist?

And here's a more practical test — since, in all probability, very few of us will be lifted from our beds tonight. Do you think that Christianity is *primarily* valuable as a means of solving our " real " problem — i.e., how to build a permanently healthy, wealthy, and wise society in *this* world? If you do, you're at least half a materialist, and someday the Marxists may be calling you comrade.

So strong is the materialist climate of opinion that even convinced Christians sometimes feel compelled to defend Christianity against the charge of " otherworldliness " — to slight its value as the passport to heaven in favor of its use-fulness as a blueprint for remodeling earth. Yet we must not blame our earthiness entirely upon Western scientific prog-ress, as if materialism had waited for Edison to invent it. B; no means. The Rome of Lucretius, the Athens of Epicurus – even the Israel of Ecclesiastes — were hardly without their ma-terialist philosophers. Devotion to the prince of this world is one of the ancient temptations, and perhaps our remote an-cestors had no sooner invented the slingshot than they reared back on their hind legs and proclaimed that their technical progress had now enabled them to do without religion. The choice before us today is just what it always was — whether to be worldly or otherworldly; whether to live for the unlov-ing self or to live for the love of God.

Judging by the Gospels, the Jews of Christ's day were nearly as worldly as we are. We have often read that they turned upon Jesus in anger; and why were they angry? It was not mere reasonless fickleness and fright; it was ma-terialism. They wanted the Messiah, yes. But what they wanted him for was to get them out of a nasty political, social, and economic hole. And when he told them, " My kingdom is not of this world," they crucified him in rage and disappoint-ment

To understand the satellite countries of the present Russian empire, we might well study the Judean province of the Roman Empire. The chosen people really were in a bad spot; some centuries of war had left them, exhausted and despair-ing, closed within the iron curtain of Rome. Their prophets told them that defeat and exile and slavery were Jehovah's punishment for disobeying the Commandments — and they drew the materialist inference that his reward for obedience would be worldly success. If they placated Spirit properly, it would shower them with gifts of matter. How could they placate that angry God? Perhaps it was then that the bitter Jewish saying, still current today, originated: " Chosen for what? Chosen for trouble! "

The Sadducees, a class of merchants grown sophisticated

through foreign trade, concluded that one ought to learn Gentile ways, since the Lord obviously favored the Gentiles. The scribes and Pharisees concluded that the Lord was a hard man at a bargain; ten commandments were too cheap a price for his help, but by hundreds of ritual observances and prohibitions and ostentatious pieties one might eventually win his favor away from the Gentiles. The ascetic Essenes, perhaps influenced by India, went into the materialism-in-reverse which considers matter altogether evil; they concluded that one should give up the life of the flesh as completely as possible. Meanwhile, what of the common people, the hewers of wood and drawers of water, the peasants and carpenters and fishermen? Why, they did what they always do — performed the labor and paid the taxes which fed the others, endured in dumb misery and hoped for a leader. It was to them that he came.

But he would not promise them worldly success. He did not organize an army to fight Caesar; instead, he told them to pay the tribute money. He did not say, "Blessed are ye when ye are rich and victorious, makers of atom bombs and policemen of the nations." He declared instead: "Blessed are ye, when men shall revile you, and persecute you, and shall say all manner of evil against you falsely, for my sake." He offered them not all the longed-for kingdoms of the earth, but only — only! — the salvation of their own souls.

They wanted him to save their lives. He said, "He that loseth his life for my sake shall find it."

This is a hard saying. It was hard for the disciples; they didn't want a suffering, dying, crucified God; they wanted a God alive and victorious, with priests and kings and Roman governors kneeling at his feet. It was hard for the martyrs; they didn't want a painful death, they wanted to be happy ordinary citizens with wives and children and a small business. And it is hard for us. We don't want a Christianity that demands we give up our lives; we'd prefer a Christianity that would show us an easy way of keeping them. Though we often couple death and resurrection in one phrase, we are seldom quite as sure of our promised resurrection as we are of our inevitable death. And we hesitate to gamble our lives on Jesus' promise.

There have always been two kinds of Christianity — man's and Christ's. Does anyone today remember how the emperor Constantine made Christianity the official religion? It is said he had a vision — saw a cross in the sky with the inscription: "In this sign shalt thou conquer." He accepted the new faith promptly, because he thought it would defeat his enemies for him. That is man's Christianity, a means to earthly triumph. And in our present crisis we are appealing to it to defeat the Russians for us. We hear of the life-and-death struggle between Christianity and Communism, the necessity of saving the world once for all, the religious duty of "keeping God alive as a social force" — as if our Lord could not survive a Soviet victory!

It is a poor sort of faith that imagines Christ defeated by anything men can do. Make no mistake: he has already survived everything we can do to him. And as for saving the world, we ought to remember that he has done that too by *his* method, not ours — the method of opening the door to the Kingdom of Heaven. Of course, God wants us to set our social house in order and to solve our economic problems. But not because he cares about house cleaning and problem-solving; because he cares about us.

There are house-proud people who will indeed sacrifice the family for the sake of the furniture. But the loving father gets the children to stop fighting and start tidying, not for the furniture's sake, but because he knows the children will be happier and better co-operating in a clean house than squabbling in a dirty one. Again: when a teacher sets her class an arithmetic problem, the pupils may imagine that all she cares about is getting the answer. Actually, however, she already knows the answer and isn't in the least interested in it; what she cares about is teaching the pupils.

Thus, while man's Christianity sometimes gets obsessed with the house and the problem, Christ's is always devoted to the children. That is the *other* Christianity, the Kingdom that is not of this world. He told us how to come out of this thick darkness into that light; it is done by loving God, and the means to *that* is loving men. So simple a statement, and yet we have found so many ways of misinterpreting it! The ages of persecution *hurt* men in the name of their love of God; fire and rack and thumbscrew were invoked to honor the Christ of mercy. In private life most of us know some brute who bullies his family and his neighbors in the name of holiness, though if Christ's prescription means anything, it surely means that you can't simultaneously love God and be nasty to your wife. But our secularist age has a pet evasion of its own; it destroys individual men in the name of its love for man.

When Christians reverse the commandment, making love of men the end and love of God only the means, they lay themselves wide open to the secularist attack. Why not, the atheist asks, bypass God altogether and love men *directly?* Thus if Latin is taught in our schools only as a means to the mastery of English, why not teach English directly and stop bothering our heads about Latin? The argument convinces many.

Life, however, answers it. The generation that is taught no Latin proves illiterate in English. The idealist who tries to love man directly soon makes the shocking discovery that men are not lovable as they are — they don't fit his ideals, so he sets up his bed of Procrustes and starts to stretch and squeeze them into a shape he likes. Usually it's the shape of a willing slave to the idealist. All the best torturers are sustained by some ideal that keeps them from noticing how nasty the reality they're making is. As a Communist once said to this writer: "Of course we're imprisoning our opponents and silencing the press and executing hostile elements. But it's only a temporary expedient, necessary to the ultimate goal!"

Such "love" is not confined to the Marxists; we see plenty of examples of it in daily life. Try to love Johnny Jones up the road, without asking God to help you, and you will discover that your defects and Johnny's both get in the way. If you're like most of us, you will overlook your own and concentrate on removing Johnny's; and he will return the compliment. Good advice will pass into argument, argument into insult — and the end is a fight, or a silent feud that may be worse, or (if you happen to be in an official position) sometimes a Johnny Jones with chunks of his brain chopped out by psychosurgery, a creature no longer human enough to resist your good intentions. You have one other alternative, if you are too kind and modest by nature for such methods — that is, to lose interest in Johnny's welfare althogether, to condone everything he does, not out of charity, but out of indifference.

The difficulty is to love men for what they are — members of yourself in the eternal body of mankind — and at the same time to make them better than they are, through love. In the famous passage of First Corinthians that defines charity, Paul describes very carefully just what is wanted, and points out that nothing else will *either* tidy up this world *or* get us into the next one. And yet minds darkened by original sin, or mental aberration, or whatever you want to call it — either way, we've all got it — cannot by an act of will achieve charity; we must acknowledge the failure of our will and ask God for help. Doesn't it seem that Christ's commandment of love involves us in a contradiction? In order to achieve the love of God, we must love our fellow men; but we *can't* love our fellow men genuinely unless we begin by loving God!

If we try to solve this paradox by intelligence, we shall be caught in it forever. But if we forget about thinking it out and start trying to live it, the paradox becomes as irrelevant as the old question, Which comes first, the chicken or the egg? How can it matter, as long as we've *got* the chickens and the eggs? Fortunately for us, we do not live by intelligence alone, for it must be admitted that in spite of nuclear physics and Yankee know-how we don't have enough of it to carry us very far. We still see through a glass darkly. Not only do we not know the nature of God; we don't even know what happens when we go to sleep. We cannot by taking thought add a cubit to our stature or keep our hearts beating. Something else does that for us; something that is not our own minds holds the universe in shape and keeps the earth going round the sun and organizes our digestive systems; and if it can do that, we may reasonably ask it to enable us to love God and man simultaneously.

The answer has come already, in the Golden Rule. Don't worry about *feeling* love; just give what you'd like to get. Suppose you were a quarrelsome little boy of eight, bent on making the world recognize your importance; how would you want to be treated? Well, treat the neighbor's bad little boy that way, next time he pulls your cat's tail. Suppose you were a nervous businessman with ulcers and a demanding daughter in an expensive college; how would you want to be treated? Well, treat your difficult partner that way. Suppose you were an irritable woman with a gland condition and a feeling that youth and beauty were slipping away and leaving you with nothing; how would you want to be treated? Well, treat your wife that way.

And suppose you were an ignorant man, half-illiterate, half-superstitious, brought to power suddenly by a revolution and constantly in terror of another revolution that might destroy you; how would you want to be treated? Would we really lose, either from the standpoint of world peace or from the standpoint of eternity, if we treated the Russian leaders that way?

We hesitate to be the *first* to apply the Golden Rule; we feel that it isn't safe, that we must wait until the whole world is ready to apply it with us. But that is why the whole world never *is* ready — they're all leaving it to the other fellow to start. Of course it isn't safe. We shall lose many worldly advantages if we love our neighbors as ourselves; we may even lose our lives. But then, that is what we were told to do.

Christ never offered us security. He left that to the politicians — Caiaphas probably offered lots of it. Christ told us to expect poverty, humiliation, persecution, and pain, and to know ourselves blessed through accepting them. The good news out of Nazareth was never reassuring news by this world's standards; reassuring news has a way of coming from the devil. For a long time we have been trying to make the best of both worlds, to accept Christianity as an ideal and materialism as a practice, and in consequence we have reached a spiritual bankruptcy in which even our journalists admit that we have no faith with which to answer the whole-souled materialism of Marx. Worldliness, we might as well admit, doesn't seem to be working so well. Perhaps it is time to revive otherworldliness? Perhaps Christ was not only a lofty idealist counseling an impractical perfection, but also the Son of God? And perhaps not only the Son of God but a practical counselor who knew what he was talking about when he talked of heaven? Perhaps it is not enough to worship him, flatter him, give his preachers money, and decorate his altar — perhaps we ought also to *obey* him?

And perhaps Christianity, if we ever embrace it not for our own worldly advantage but through surrender to God, will not only enable us to obey the Ten Commandments but enable us to enjoy it; not only save this transitory world for the few perplexed years we spend in it, but bring us out of this noise and darkness and helplessness and terror that we call the world into the full Light: Light we remember from our childhood dreams, and from glimpses through music and art and the ecstasy of first love; Light we have known through a brief glow in our few moments of really selfless charity; Light which, in our secret hearts, we desire more than money and sex and power and the pride of the self. We men are all thieves who have stolen the self which was meant as a part of God and tried to keep it for ourselves alone. But if we give it up again, we might hear the words he spoke to a penitent thief once: " To-day shalt thou be with me in paradise."

JOY DAVIDMAN

Joy Davidman, poet, novelist, and religious writer, was born in New York City in 1915. Educated in New York, she received the B.A. degree from Hunter College in 1934 and the M.A. from Columbia University in 1935. She specialized in the study of English literature and taught English in New York high schools, 1935–1938. In one year, 1938, she won both the Yale Series of Younger Poets award and the Russell Loines Award of the National Institute of Arts and Sciences. In 1939 she worked as a screenwriter in Hollywood for Metro-Goldwyn-Mayer. She married William Lindsay Gresham in 1942, and two children were born to them: David, in 1944, and Douglas, in 1945.

Her published books, besides *Smoke on the Mountain*, include two volumes of verse, *Letter to a Comrade* (Yale Series of Younger Poets, Yale University Press, 1938) and *War Poems of the United Nations*, an anthology (Dial Press, 1944), and two novels, *Anya* and *Weeping Bay* (Macmillan Company, 1940 and 1950).

Joy Davidman was converted from communism to Christianity, in part as a result of reading the writings of C. S. Lewis. After her divorce from Gresham she went to England and served as Lewis's secretary. Shortly before they were married in 1957 it was discovered that she had cancer. She died in June, 1960. As he dealt with his intense grief Lewis recorded his feelings in a series of notebooks, which were published under a pseudonym as *A Grief Observed* (1963). Current editions appear under Lewis's name.